ONE MINUTE WITH THE WOMEN OF THE BIBLE

ELIZABETH GEORGE

HARVEST HOUSE PUBLISHERS
EUGENE, OREGON

Cover by Dugan Design Group

ONE MINUTE WITH THE WOMEN OF THE BIBLE
Adapted from *Walking with the Women of the Bible*
Copyright © 1999 by Elizabeth George
Published 2016 by Harvest House Publishers
Eugene, Oregon 97402
www.harvesthousepublishers.com

ISBN: 978-0-7369-6971-0 (Milano Softone™)
ISBN: 978-0-7369-6972-7 (eBook)

Library of Congress Cataloging-in-Publication Data
    George, Elizabeth, 1944-
    [Women who loved God]
    Walking with the women of the Bible / Elizabeth George.
        p. cm.
    Originally published: Women who loved God. Eugene, Or. : Harvest House, c1999.
    ISBN 978-0-7369-2377-4 (pbk.)
    1. Women—Prayers and devotions. 2. Women in the Bible—Meditations. I. Title.
    BV4844.G433 2008
    242'.643—dc22

                                                2007039196

Printed in China

        17 18 19 20 21 22 23 24 / RDS-JC / 10 9 8 7 6 5 4 3 2

Contents

*D*o you love God and want to know more about Him? About how He helps and sustains His people...including you? Are you looking for ways to handle hard times? Guidelines for making better decisions? Or are you unsure how to live out your love for Him? Perhaps you'd like a mentor—a woman who's followed Jesus for a long time and wants to help you in your faith walk?

Through insightful readings focused on the women of the Bible you'll discover how God leads, encourages, uses, and works in the lives of people. Written just for you, these devotions are for today's woman and are practical, helpful, and hands on. The women in God's Word have shown me—and they'll show you too—how to live out the Lord's plan and will right now...today! I'll also share the wisdom He's taught me through my many years of living for Him. Together we'll explore how to follow and serve Him wholeheartedly, how to love others more thoroughly, how to strengthen our trust in Him, and how to put wings on our dreams. We'll come alongside these women and discover the characteristics and gifts that flourish in women who follow God: purpose, devotion, trust, courage, hope, wisdom, blessing, and faithfulness.

May your journey to greater faith be filled with joy, delight, and adventure each step of the way. You'll never be the same after walking with the women of the Bible!

Your friend in Him,

Elizabeth George

Purpose for a Lifetime

1 Eve

Reflecting God's Glory

God created man in His own image.
GENESIS 1:27

*D*o *you know you were created in the image of God?*
When God created woman, He created her in His image. Let this sink into your heart and mind. You are creative, intelligent, and rational because you were created in God's image.

Do you know you are a reflection of God's glory? That's what being created in His image means. You reflect Him to other people. Every time you reach out in love, perform a deed of kindness, soften your heart in forgiveness, show a little extra patience, and follow through in faithfulness, other people experience the character of God through you.

Do you know you are created to have fellowship and communion with God? "God is faithful, by whom you were called into the fellowship of His Son, Jesus Christ our Lord" (1 Corinthians 1:9).

As a reflection of God's glory, thank God and…

Resolve never to criticize or downgrade yourself, but instead

Rejoice that you are fearfully and wonderfully made.

Resolve to walk by faith paths you may not understand and

Rejoice in the promise of His nearness as He directs your way.

Resolve to live as a child of God through His Son, Jesus Christ, and

Rejoice that as God's child your name is written in heaven.

Resolve to commune with God daily through prayer and Bible study, and

Rejoice in His strength each day and hope in Him for tomorrow.

Resolve to reflect His glory and

Rejoice in His love!

Eve

Fairest of Creation

Male and female He created them.
GENESIS 1:27

God was busy for six days creating His beautiful new world. The stage was set. The Creator's magnificent scenery was finished and in place. His sun, moon, and stars lit up His perfect planet. All creatures great and small enjoyed a perfect environment. Yet God wasn't quite finished. At last He presented His masterpieces to the rest of nature. First the man, Adam. Then—finally and dramatically—the woman, Eve.

Devised by a perfect God, Eve reflected His divine perfection in her femaleness. Created for a position of honor, woman was born to life's loveliest, most lofty throne of glory—"the glory of man" (1 Corinthians 11:7). What can you do to revel in your femaleness?

- *Accept your femininity.* There's no need to feel inferior, second-class, or second-rate. Woman was God's last creation. After God presented woman He proclaimed His creation "very good." Adam and

Eve were alike, yet different. One was male and one female. Together as well as individually they reflected God's image and glory.

- *Embrace your womanhood.* Own your loveliness, your uniqueness, your beauty as a female. Delight yourself in God's handiwork—in being a woman.

- *Cultivate your femininity.* This book is about the gracious, glorious, beautiful, prized-by-God women of the Bible. As you read, allow God's truths to permeate your understanding. You are of very high value to Him!

- *Excel in your role as a woman.* As God's woman, purpose to be the best of the best. Delight in His perfect design, in His good and acceptable and perfect will for your life. He created you as a woman. As such, you join Eve's exalted position of "fairest of creation." [1]

Pass It On

Eve...was the mother of all living.

GENESIS 3:20

*G*uilty!" God pronounced after Adam's wife listened to the tempter, ate of the forbidden tree, and involved her husband in rebellion. It reverberated in Eve's heart and mind. There was no doubt about her guilt. But as darkness settled in, she heard Adam declare, "Your name shall be called 'Eve...the mother of all living.'" With these words Eve glimpsed a fresh ray of light.

Having been given a name filled with promise, Eve realized she, the guilty sinner, could still serve her gracious and forgiving God. How? By bearing Adam's children and becoming the mother of many generations (1 Corinthians 11:12). Her name reflected the role she would play in spiritual history.

"Eve." From death sprang life. From darkness, light. From the curse, a blessing. From a sentence of death, hope for the future. From the stinging despair of defeat, the strength of budding faith. Eve was the mother of all living!

Do you know your life counts too? True, you share

Eve's sentence of physical death (Romans 5:12). But you also have life to give and pass on. How?

- You give life through your physical efforts to care for others.

- You share spiritual life by telling others about Jesus.

- You are the life of your home, bringing the sparkle of laughter and joy to other people.

- You pass physical life on to your children.

- You can pass the potential for eternal life on to your children by teaching them the gospel of Jesus Christ.

Feed your spiritual life by sending your roots deep into God's love. The energy of life, the purpose of life, all you have of life to pass on is from the Lord!

Sailing into God's Plan

> *I will establish my covenant with*
> *you...and your wife.*
> GENESIS 6:18 NIV

*W*e don't know her name so let's call her "Mrs. Noah." She spent her days loving her husband, Noah, raising their three sons, and caring for their home. Daily life was simple...until "the call" came from the Lord.

Grieved over the wickedness of mankind, God decided to destroy humans, the animals of the fields, and the birds of the air. Because Noah trusted and walked with God, God chose to save him and his family and told him to make an ark.

As Noah moved forward in obedience, Mrs. Noah may have mused, *What can I do? How can I help my husband fulfill God's plan?*

Pray. She could pray for mankind as God's judgment loomed, for her husband as he served the Lord, and for her family to also follow God.

Encourage. Husbands thrive on their wives' cheerful, hope-filled words of support. She could encourage Noah in his work.

Believe. She may have wondered about the ark and the possibility of a flood, but she could choose to believe.

Help. She could help with the animals and gather the food they'd need for their mysterious voyage of faith.

Follow. She could—by faith—follow her husband's leading day by day for 120 years, the 43,800 days it took to complete the ark…right into the ark of salvation that transported her family into an unknown future.

> *Lord, I want to have faith that prays persistently, chooses righteousness, encourages fellow believers, helps Your kingdom, and follows You faithfully. Help me find strength for today and hope for tomorrow as I sail into the future You have for me.*

Sarai/Sarah

Believing One More Time

Sarai was barren; she had no child.
GENESIS 11:30

*S*arai was barren; she had no child." Seven words. A simple statement of cold, hard fact. Perhaps Sarai (whom God later called Sarah) wondered, *What's gone wrong? What have I done? Why hasn't God blessed me with children?* On and on her questioning went...and so did her pain. Nothing could relieve it, soothe it, take it away. Childlessness was a stigma that seared deeply into her soul with each childless sunrise.

Sarah was the wife of Abram (whose name was changed to Abraham) and a follower of God. She was barren for many years, but then God promised Abraham and Sarah a child in their old age. But the baby was a long time coming. With aching heart and stinging tears, Sarah trusted God one more time, for one more day, over and over. Despite a few setbacks, Sarah learned that faith—instead of giving up, succumbing to bitterness, lashing out at others, turning her back on God, giving in to a contentious spirit,

16

and manipulating the situation—is the best way to face the distresses of life.

For 11 years Sarah grabbed on to God's promise. That's more than 4000 "faith reaches"! Then God's promise was fulfilled and Isaac was born. Oh, how Abraham and Sarah must have rejoiced!

Faith, like physical muscle, is developed and strengthened with use. Each time you trust God as you face seemingly unbearable, unusual, unchangeable circumstances, your faith increases. What difficult issue are you facing today? Reach out to God one more time! Turn toward the unknown, the unseen, the eternal, and watch your faith grow.

Sarah

Faith Means Moving Forward

[Abraham] took [Sarah] his wife...to the land of Canaan.

GENESIS 12:5

"Oh, the heartache! Will it ever go away?" Perhaps these words darkened Sarah's thoughts the day she followed her full-of-faith husband out of Haran. Leaving Haran was bad enough, but going to the land of Canaan made it even worse! Canaan was 600 miles away from her family and friends. Abraham had announced they were going to Nowhere Land, as far as Sarah was concerned.

Just when Sarah was getting used to Nowhere Land, a famine struck and they had to move to Egypt—300 miles away! *Oh, if only I were still in Haran,* Sarah may have thought.

Backward gazes can be dangerous and impede spiritual growth. So how can we look forward and faithfully follow God when circumstances are bad? Here's a great acronym!

Face forward. Real life happens in the present, and God's blessings happen now and in the future.

Accept your circumstances. God uses the difficulties of life to help you mature and grow in Him.

If you're following God, you will find Him in all your circumstances.

Trust in the Lord. God will keep you in perfect peace when your mind is focused on Him.

Hope for the future. God is a bright star who will light your path in the present darkness.

> *Dear God of Sarai,*
> *grant that such a one as I*
> *may see the good in bad*
> *and the faith to be had...*
> *following Thee!*

7 Hagar

An Encouragement and Blessing

The Angel of the Lord found her.
GENESIS 16:7

*A*braham and his wife, Sarah, certainly led interesting lives. Although they both followed God, they were human and made mistakes. But God still promised them a child in their old age. Sarah, long barren, became impatient and decided to "help" God by having her maid, Hagar, bear Abraham's child.

Hagar was pregnant, but things weren't turning out like Sarah planned. Hagar now despised Sarah and lorded it over her. Maybe she flaunted her ability to get pregnant. Maybe she ordered Sarah about because she was pregnant with Abraham's child. Sarah finally had enough. She checked with Abraham, and then treated Hagar harshly.

Hagar decided to run away, living up to the meaning of her name—"flight." She ran into the wilderness, her emotions reeling.

But God was watching over Hagar and Abraham's

unborn child. He sent an angel to comfort this distraught woman. Through the angel Hagar received from God:

- *Instructions.* For her safety and well-being—and the baby's too—she was told to return to Sarah. There Hagar would receive food, water, shelter, and help.

- *Encouragement.* The angel told her she would bear a son. Even though life was bleak now, she would one day have a son, have a family.

- *A promise.* God would multiply Hagar's descendants. Although Hagar was a servant, she would become the mother of many.

What an encouragement and blessing for Hagar!

Do you need encouragement? A fresh, shining vision of hope? Spend time with God...talking and listening. Read His "letters" to you—the Bible—for His promises, wisdom, and instructions.

Sarah

Promoted for a Purpose

You shall not call her name Sarai.
GENESIS 17:15

*I*n biblical times a name change essentially meant a "promotion"—a recognition of new status. And like in school, promotions had to be earned. Required courses must be successfully completed before a diploma is delivered. Genesis 17 offers a snapshot of Sarah's promotion in the school of faith. God said to Abraham, "As for Sarai...you shall not call her name Sarai, but Sarah shall be her name. And I will bless her and also give you a son by her; then I will bless her, and she shall be a mother of nations."

What courses did Sarah complete to qualify for promotion? As you read along, grade yourself in the blanks provided.

- *Sarah followed her husband.* She trusted Abraham as he followed God. Her life was filled with moves and changes, but she accepted her lifestyle as God's will and her husband as God's instrument in her life. _____

- *Sarah trusted God.* She almost failed the course, but God's love covered her mistakes. She grew in faith as she hoped...prayed...and trusted God. _____

- *Sarah waited on God.* Actually, she was still learning to wait. Sarah was getting the instruction she needed to continue her long wait for the son God promised. Waiting was never easy for Sarah. _____

- *Sarah developed a gentle and quiet spirit.* "Sarai" carried the connotation of "contention" as well as "princess," and she was certainly contentious at times. But Sarah eventually adorned herself with the kind of spirit that pleases God (1 Peter 3:4-5). _____

How'd you do? And what steps can you take to grow in these areas? Write them down and get started on them today! Continue to move forward in God's school of faith.

Awaiting Future Promises

I will bless her and...give you a son by her.
GENESIS 17:16

*H*ow many times had it happened? Sarah could count at least five times when God promised Abraham a son, a seed, an offspring—and still she wasn't pregnant! For a while they thought Ishmael, Abraham's son with Hagar, was "the son of promise." But God told Abraham, "Sarah your wife shall bear you a son." This time God mentioned Sarah specifically. No wonder Abraham fell down because he was laughing so hard. Sarah was 90 years old!

With her new name shining bright, Sarah undoubtedly wanted her deepening faith to be equally brilliant. But did she wonder, just like God's people do sometimes, how to believe in God's promises when situations seem impossible and the waiting never-ending? Scripture is full of suggestions for maintaining faith.

> *By choice.* The opposite of faith is disbelief or doubt. When God presents one of His dazzling promises, He offers you the choice

of accepting its dazzling brilliance or smothering it in a dark cloud of doubt.

By faith. Strength for today and hope for tomorrow are realized by putting your trust and faith in God's promises. Look for God's handiwork and His answers to your questions. Enjoy His strength and hope.

By exercise. Faith is like a muscle. Through exercise it gradually increases in strength and size. When you choose to believe God and His promises and live accordingly, your faith is exercised and you grow stronger.

Is there an area of your life that stretches your faith? Do you have a physical problem like Sarah? A family problem? A personal struggle? A financial test? Exercise your faith! Push through any uncertainty and focus on the One whose promises never fail.

Your Lasting Legacy

She shall be a mother of nations.
GENESIS 17:16

*G*od said of Sarah, "She shall be a mother of nations; kings of peoples shall be from her." In time, Sarah's ancestors became "as the stars of the heaven and as the sand which is on the seashore." The roll call of Sarah's descendants includes great patriarchs of the faith, kings, and the Savior of the world, Jesus Christ—and continues right on down to you if you've been born spiritually into the line of Abraham through Christ (Romans 4:16-25). The lowly Sarah, pilgrim from Ur and stranger in Canaan, became the progenitor of all the saints through the ages!

Another woman will also be a mother of nations. Who? You! As you faithfully teach your children the life-saving, life-giving truths of Scripture, you invite your children into God's family. As you pass on the gospel to your beloved children, they can, in turn, pass it on to the next generation. Your godly influence will continue through time and through generations as innumerable as the stars and the sand!

Are you thinking, *But I don't have children. This doesn't apply to me*? Oh, but it does! By sharing the life-changing truth about Jesus with coworkers, neighbors, and family members you give people the opportunity to be born spiritually in Him. You have so much to offer to others. Don't waste a moment of your faith stewardship. Pass it on!

Blessings Will Come

At the appointed time...Sarah shall have a son.

GENESIS 18:14

*T*here is no such thing as "time wasted"...if you're waiting on the Lord. Sarah, the woman God called "a mother of nations," waited on the Lord's promise of a son for 25 years—and way past her childbearing years. Amid her strong faith Sarah experienced moments of doubt. *Is the promise real? Is God going to follow through?*

Few things are tougher than waiting on God's timing—His "appointed time." Yet we're all enrolled in God's School of Waiting. He uses this time to teach and transform us. But He also blesses us! Look for these special gifts and savor them.

> *Blessing #1: Increased value.* Waiting increases the value and importance of what you're waiting for. Whether it's being delivered from suffering, discovering God's purpose, waiting for direction, clearing up confusion, affording

a new home, getting married, attending a family reunion, anticipating a prodigal's return or a child's birth, waiting makes the desired object or event a greater treasure when it finally occurs.

Blessing #2: Increased time. While we're waiting God gives us the precious gift of time—time to embrace life's circumstances, to press closer to God's loving and understanding heart, to grow in the grace of patience, to encourage others who also experience the pain of waiting.

Blessing #3: Increased faith. Faith grows and is strengthened through time. And when the time of waiting is done and God blesses you with fulfillment, what a time for rejoicing! And this results in even deeper faith!

Sounds of Joy

God has made me laugh.
GENESIS 21:6

The tent rang with sounds of joy. Sarah and Abraham couldn't contain their glee as they held their promised son. Sarah's shameful barrenness had ended! Finally—after 25 years, after hearing the promise again and again, after a visit from God and two angels—little Isaac, soft and wrinkled, was born to the weathered and wrinkled parents. In their exultant joy they named the babe Isaac, meaning "he laughs."

Sarah marveled, "Who would have said to Abraham that Sarah would nurse children? For I have borne him a son in his old age." God, who is always fully able, provided a miracle. Now instead of her being scorned, people would join her in rejoicing. Isaac was the child of her own body, the child of her old age, the child of God's promise, the fruit of tested faith, the gift of God's grace, and the heaven-appointed heir to Abraham. Can you imagine Sarah's jubilant heart song?

Why not join Sarah in a chorus of praise? Even if life

is difficult right now, lift your voice in joy because of the hope you have in Christ. Rejoice that either here or in heaven, depending on God's appointed time, you'll experience the full, unimaginable blessing of His wonderful promises completely fulfilled. Sing with the psalmist in wonderful anticipation:

> Weeping may remain for a night, but rejoicing comes in the morning...You turned my wailing into dancing; you removed my sackcloth and clothed me with joy (Psalm 30:5, 11 NIV).

Spiritual joy is not an emotion. It's a response to a Spirit-filled life (Galatians 5:22). Can you "count it all joy when you fall into various trials" (James 1:2)? By an act of faith, resolve to be joyous in your present difficulty.

13   Hagar

Empowered with Belief

Fear not.

Genesis 21:17

After Isaac, Abraham and Sarah's son, was born, there was great rejoicing. But Hagar, the mother of Abraham's son Ishmael, refused to join in. Because of her ever-present negative attitude, Sarah asked Abraham to send Hagar and Ishmael away. Upset, Abraham consulted God, who told him to do as Sarah asked. But He also assured Abraham that He would watch over Ishmael. So Abraham told Hagar she and her son had to leave (Genesis 21).

In the desert their water supply ran out, and Hagar and Ishmael were dying of dehydration. The best Hagar could do was thrust her son under the scant shade of a desert scrub, drag herself away from his pathetic sobs, and weep while she waited for death to come. Suddenly, booming out of the heavens, came the voice of an angel: "Fear not, for God has heard the voice of the lad." How encouraged Hagar must have been!

What are your favorite "fear nots" in the Bible? Does your list include these from the King James Version?

> "Fear not...I am thy shield" (Genesis 15:1).

> "Fear not...for I am with thee" (Genesis 26:24).

> "Fear ye not, stand still, and see the salvation of the LORD" (Exodus 14:13).

Any conflict is won up front when you "fear not." So don the armor of the biblical "fear nots." They'll form an effective, protective covering against fear. Memorize or write them down and keep them handy so they'll always be ready to use. "God has not given us a spirit of fear, but of power and of love and of a sound mind" (2 Timothy 1:7). Praise His wonderful name!

Hagar

Do Something!

Arise, lift up the lad.

GENESIS 21:18

*J*n the life story of Hagar, God presents a powerful, two-step plan for successfully enduring distresses and overcoming the obstacles of life:

Step 1—a negative command: Fear not!

Step 2—a positive command: Do something!

Hagar's energy was spent and so was her faith when God issued His Step 1 order. Calling out to Hagar as she and her son awaited death in the desert, the angel of the Lord commanded, "Fear not!"

Next God delivered Step 2: "Arise!" In other words, "Do something! Put feet on your faith." God's message was, "Don't give up—get up! Continue. Move. Muster your energy. Take action!"

Why a call to action? Because action—continuing to do what you can—helps you conquer depression, stave off defeat, shake off despair, and vanquish discouragement.

What challenges are in your path today? Are you facing a hopeless situation? Insurmountable odds? A disaster?

Tune your ear and your heart and your strength to God's voice of wisdom. He says, "Arise...move...do something!" Ask Him for wisdom and guidance and then plan your day. Make a to-do list. Get off the couch or out of bed. Commit to life. To reaching forward. To attaining the "prize of the high calling of God in Christ Jesus" (Philippians 3:14). Tap into the strength promised to you in Christ.

Take on a "go get 'em" attitude and posture. Act! A law of physics states, "A body at rest tends to remain at rest, and a body in motion tends to remain in motion." So move!

Doing something is great advice, but there is one caution to heed. Make sure your movement is in God's direction. Read His Word. Seek godly counsel. Then with God's leading, move out with purpose.

15 Hagar

God's Plentiful Provision

And she saw a well of water.
GENESIS 21:19

The God who provides reached out and helped Hagar and her son as they were dying in the desert. God heard their cries and met their needs and encouraged and instructed them. But He didn't stop there!

Promise—Indicating all was not lost for her son, God promised Hagar, "I will make him a great nation." When no ray of hope was evident, God gave this mother a promise to cling to.

> Whatever your life situation, you've been promised "all things that pertain to life" (2 Peter 1:3). You can go through life fueled by God's promise of faithfulness.

Guidance—Whether Hagar looked to God or not, God looked to her—and looked out for her. "God opened her eyes" and directed her to a nearby spring. He led Hagar, blinded by fear and exhaustion, safely to water.

God delights in leading you. He is constantly available to guide you through the events and circumstances of your life. He is the Good Shepherd who leads His sheep (Psalm 23).

Provision—When God opened Hagar's eyes, she saw a well. In her frightening plight, God provided a spring, a fountain, a source of life!

Your promise for today—and every day—is God's guidance and His plentiful provision as you walk in His ways.

Sarah

Embracing the Seasons of Life

Sarah lived one hundred and twenty-seven years.

GENESIS 23:1

*S*arah is the only woman in the Bible whose actual age is given. She lived 127 years. What seasons did she go through in those years?

First, a season of leaving. How hard it was for Sarah to leave the prosperous, culturally advanced metropolis of Ur, situated along the lush Euphrates River valley, to go to Haran (Genesis 11)! And then God, through her husband, Abraham, asked her to leave Haran to go into the arid desert.

Second, a season of learning. Sarah's lessons included following her husband. For 60 long years they never settled down for long. And there was also Sarah's often-repeated assignment of trusting God in His promise of a son. During 25 years of waiting, her faith surged and waned. The agony of time passing by was especially difficult for Sarah.

Third, a season of leaning. Sarah was taken into harems twice. Out of fear, Abraham told the Egyptian Pharaoh, "She is my sister," so Pharaoh took her to the palace. Later Abraham repeated this deceit to King Abimelech, who also took Sarah home. Cut off from her husband, Sarah leaned on God. She discovered, as the psalmist did, that "God is our refuge and strength, a very present help in trouble" (Psalm 46:1).

Finally, a season of loving. In His goodness and at His appointed time, God gifted the 90-year-old Sarah with Isaac, her very own baby! How she must have cherished every second of the 37 years she was privileged to be a loving mother.

Did you notice Sarah's "seasons" had nothing to do with her age? They had to do with her situation and attitude. What season are you in today? Trust God for His purpose and His perfect plan.

Making Time Count

So Sarah died.

GENESIS 23:2

*A*s one wedding ceremony puts it, marriage lasts "until death parts the partners." The day arrived when Sarah, faithful wife to Abraham, slipped away. But death is the doorway to eternal life for God's saints.

How many times have you thought about death? And does your perspective match what God says about death? Note these truths.

> *Truth #1.* How you die is as important as how you live. "For if we live, we live to the Lord; and if we die, we die to the Lord" (Romans 14:8). Face death boldly with unfailing courage. Your goal is to glorify and exalt Christ by your life and through your death.

> *Truth #2.* How you view death is important. The world views death as the end, as the entrance into something unknown, as something awful, something to be feared. But for God's

people, "to die is gain" (Philippians 1:21). As someone pointed out, "God strips me of everything to give me everything!"

Truth #3. How you define death is important. In Philippians 1:23 Paul describes death as departing and being with Christ. The imagery used is one of loosening the ropes on a tent, pulling up the tent stakes, and moving on. Each day brings you closer to the exchange of this imperfect life for residence in a world of glory.

Do you know the hour of your death? No. But death is certain. So what can you do each day to ensure your life is meaningful? Model Christ. Share Him with family and friends. Be faithful to God. Make time count!

Devotion of the Heart

A Remarkable Name and Legacy

Milcah, the wife of Nahor...
GENESIS 24:15

Her name is listed in God's Word, but there is very little detail about the life of Milcah. What can we piece together?

- Her name means queen.
- Her father was Haran, the father of Abraham.
- Her brother was Abraham, friend of God.
- Her sister-in-law was Sarah, a beautiful woman of faith.
- Her husband was Nahor, brother to Abraham.
- Her children included eight sons.
- Her lovely granddaughter was Rebekah, who later married Isaac.

How can you follow in Milcah's steps?

Be faithful to God. When Abraham needed a godly wife for his Isaac—the son from whom the entire Jewish race would arise—he knew she would be among the offspring of Milcah.

Be faithful to your husband. Over the years Milcah must have steadfastly loved and served her husband through thick and thin.

Be faithful to raise your children God's way. Eight sons are listed to Milcah's credit. Her son Bethuel fathered Rebekah, who married the patriarch Isaac.

Milcah lived up to her regal name in bearing and dignity. She helped establish a godly seed in a godless world.

Faithfulness is the training ground for greater service. How can you show faithfulness today?

19 Rebekah

Dedicated to God

The daughter of Bethuel...
GENESIS 24:24

*W*e meet only a handful of single women in Scripture. In Genesis 24 God presents Rebekah, a woman of stunning faith and service. What qualities make her one of God's special servants?

- *Purity*—She was chaste until marriage.
- *Industriousness*—Rather than looking for a husband or moping and mourning over the lack of one, Rebekah served her family and others.
- *Hospitality*—Her home was open to those who needed care.
- *Energy*—Abundant activity is a sign of happiness, and Rebekah had energy to spare as she went extra miles to serve people.

If you're a single woman, God has a beautiful plan for you. He encourages you to remain "holy both in body and in spirit." You also have more time to serve God because you're not distracted by a husband or children. As you use the same qualities Rebekah had to fully engage in "the things of the Lord" (1 Corinthians 7:34), you'll be given glorious opportunities to help others.

Is singleness a reality for you today? Although you may desire to be married, while you wait for God's leading in that area, dedicate yourself to God and give yourself whole-heartedly to His service and His cause.

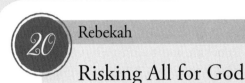

Risking All for God

[God] will send His angel before you.
GENESIS 24:7

*H*ow does a man find a wife? This was the predicament Abraham was in. But the wife he needed to find was not for himself. She was for his only son, 37-year-old Isaac. "Who?" and "How?" were questions that probably plagued Abraham.

Realizing that the continuation of his family line and the fulfillment of God's promise to make his family a great nation were at stake, Abraham called in his oldest servant, the faithful Eliezer. After receiving a solemn oath from Eliezer, Abraham sent this 85-year-old servant on a 500-mile journey to find a wife for Isaac. This woman would have to be willing to follow Eliezer back to an unfamiliar land and marry a man she'd never met! What requirements did God and Abraham have for Isaac's future wife?

- *She must not be a Canaanite.* A wife from godless people could influence Isaac and his offspring away from the true God.

- *She must be from Abraham's family.* He instructed Eliezer, "You shall go to my country and to my family."
- *She must be willing to follow Eliezer back to the land of Abraham and Isaac.* A woman who would do this would be a woman willing to forsake all—in faith—for the glorious future God had ordained.

Actively follow with all your heart, soul, mind, and strength the God of the Bible and embrace His standards. You will have a tremendous influence on your world, your friends, your husband, your children, and your extended family. Let God's light shine!

The Beauty of Diligence

Rebekah...came out with her pitcher.
Genesis 24:15

*M*ost people tend to evaluate a person's character based on their first meeting. First impressions make such an impact. It was no different when Abraham's servant first saw Rebekah. Tired from the long journey, Eliezer waited by the town well in Nahor for the young women to come draw water. He prayed, asking God to bring the right woman for Isaac and have her offer him a drink of water. Before he'd finished speaking, "Behold, Rebekah...came out with her pitcher on her shoulder."

Eliezer saw right away that Rebekah was a working woman. Probably twice a day she took a heavy clay pitcher to the town's water source to draw precious water and carry it home. What can we surmise about her?

See her beautiful qualities of diligence and faithfulness. Watch carefully her tireless industry and humble willingness to engage in menial work. Observe her ability to do demanding work. Marvel at her servant heart that placed the needs of her family above any concern about what others might think.

Do you view menial work as degrading? Do you think physical work is done by other people and not you? Do you dread rolling up your sleeves and working on "necessary but thankless" tasks? In His Word God praises the enchanting-but-industrious Rebekah. So if you're tempted to put off or disdain difficult work, look to this beautiful woman for courage and example. Also read about the woman of Proverbs 31, "She girds herself with strength, and strengthens her arms...Strength and honor are her clothing" (Proverbs 31:17,25).

What can you do to help and influence the people God puts in your life? Does your church need your energy working with children or in Sunday school or in the office? Be willing to work, and see where you can serve today.

Gracious Giving

I will draw water for your camels also.
Genesis 24:19

esus told people, "Whoever compels you to go one mile, go with him two. Give to him who asks you" (Matthew 5:41-42). Thousands of years before God's Son uttered these words, the young woman Rebekah was putting the principle into practice.

Picture an old man and 10 thirsty camels lingering around a well in a dusty, arid city of Mesopotamia. The elderly Eliezer traveled 500 miles to find a wife for his master's son. "O Lord God...please give me success this day," the tired servant prayed. Before he added an "amen" to his request, a beautiful young woman came to the well to draw water.

Eliezer hurried to meet the woman and said, "Please let down your pitcher that I may drink." How did the beautiful Rebekah respond? Gracious and helpful, she said, "Drink, my lord." And then she volunteered to take care of the 10 camels!

Do you wonder how many draws of water from the

well Rebekah had to make to satisfy those thirsty camels? A camel can drink as much as 25 gallons after a long journey! The generous, energetic Rebekah probably hastened back and forth from the well to the water trough many times to satiate the weary animals. Rebekah went "many extra miles" on that extraordinary day.

No price can be put on the sterling qualities Rebekah exhibited in her attitudes and actions that day by the well. Her servant spirit shone like the sun, revealing her sincere and good heart. She was respectful, aware of those in need, willing to help, generous, and tireless. Giving drink to the tired old man met only one of his needs, so Rebekah expanded her care to include his animals.

Today why not follow beautiful Rebekah's footsteps and be on the lookout for a needy person you can help? And then with a heart of helping do more than is needed.

Open Your Heart... and Your Home

We have...room to lodge.

GENESIS 24:25

braham's servant Eliezer traveled hundreds of miles in the desert climate. As he prayed beside a town well, the lovely young Rebekah appeared. After first drawing water from the cistern to satisfy his thirst—and even taking care of the camels' thirst—Rebekah respectfully answered the man's questions regarding who she was and whether her family had a place for him to stay. In her welcoming way, Rebekah replied with her name and an invitation for food, lodging, and fodder for the animals. Inside Rebekah's family home, Eliezer would be the recipient of assistance, refreshment, shelter, and rest.

Do you see your home as a gift from God to be used for the comfort and well-being of others? A Christian home is earth's sweetest picture of heaven and a welcome relief in our stressed and weary society. Open your arms and your heart to those in need. Consider missionaries who, like

Eliezer, travel long distances and are in need of the necessities of life—food and a place to rest their weary bodies. Befriend a college student who would thrive on time spent in your home. Ponder the needs of a widow or widower who has no one to talk to. Count the singles you know who are on their own.

Why not serve a meal to a neighbor who is searching for answers? Or have tea with a brokenhearted mother struggling over her child. Offer a listening ear, an encouraging word, and a heartfelt prayer with those in need. Hospitality is a matter of the heart—your heart. All who enter your door offer you opportunities to minister. Welcome them into your home sweet home—a home where Jesus lives in the heart of the hostess.

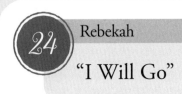

24 Rebekah

"I Will Go"

And she said, "I will go."
GENESIS 24:58

alk is one thing. Action is another. And action has always been a measure of true faith. Rebekah's faith was demonstrated when she took a gigantic leap in trusting God.

The progression of events that led to that giant step of faith began when Abraham told his servant Eliezer to go to his relatives and find a wife for his son Isaac. When Eliezer reached his destination, the beautiful Rebekah, daughter of Abraham's distant relative Bethuel, invited him to stay in her family's home. While there, her father and brother agreed that Rebekah would marry Isaac.

However, when talk turned to a departure date for their cherished Rebekah, her mother and brother said, "Let the young woman stay with us a few days, at least ten; after that she may go." When Eliezer said he needed to return home, they said, "We will call the young woman and ask her personally." When they asked her, "Will you go with this man?" the question really was "Will you go now or wait?"

Rebekah's remarkable faith was evident as she stated, "I will go." She was basically saying, "I will go...with a stranger...to live in an unknown land...to be the wife of an unknown man. I will go...even though I will probably never see my family again...even though I have no time to prepare...even though the nomadic life of Abraham's family will be strenuous. I will go!"

Take a quick inventory of your life. Is there any act of faith you're postponing—even for a few days? Any decision you're putting off? Waiting may be easier, but the harder path of faith in action promises greater blessings. Delayed obedience is really disobedience, and delayed action puts off God's blessings. Step out in faith today.

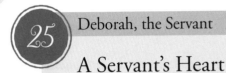
A Servant's Heart

*So they sent away Rebekah...and her
nurse.*

GENESIS 24:59

*T*he Christian life is one of selfless service to others, and
one picture in particular is worth a thousand words
when it comes to understanding what this looks like in
God's eyes. Deborah, Rebekah's lifelong servant, offers a
beautiful portrait of devoted service.

As a bond servant, Deborah was obligated to perform—
without question or delay—her mistress' will. Whatever
the order, Deborah was to do it quickly, quietly, without
question. For Deborah that job description meant leaving the home she had always known to journey 500 miles
with Rebekah to her new home—and doing so immediately! While Rebekah's family talked about this surprising
turn of events, Deborah was trying to adjust to the idea
that in the morning she too was leaving forever. And she
was probably busily packing for both of them.

Deborah is a study in diligence as well as service. Her
name, in fact, means "bee," suggesting industry and

usefulness. We can imagine she was constantly active and ever caring.

You too are called to serve people. How can you be industrious and willing like Deborah? Try these tactics.

- *Tackle your work energetically.* Whatever chore you face, do it with all your might and with a mind to work. Do your work heartily and for the Lord, not to individuals.

- *Tackle your work joyfully.* Choose to work with a joyful heart as well as a servant heart. You'll find more satisfaction when you approach work as a labor of love.

Since you're ultimately serving God in your work, develop a positive attitude and do the best you can. How is your energy level and attitude when you're home? That is where your greatest industry and joy needs to be focused.

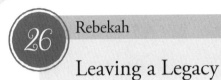

Leaving a Legacy

And they blessed Rebekah.
GENESIS 24:60

Twenty-four hours ago life had been so different for Rebekah and her family. An ordinary trip to the well changed the course of their history and, in fact, the history of the world. The young woman Rebekah had simply gone, as she did every day, to draw water for the household. Yet on that God-appointed day, a stranger was waiting, a foreigner sent by their kinsman Abraham to find a bride for his son Isaac.

Dear, kind Rebekah gave the servant water and invited him to her family home for the night. Over dinner her father and brother agreed that Rebekah was the woman God had chosen to marry Abraham's heir. As the sun rose the next morning, Rebekah mounted one of the stranger's camels and left for the mysterious, faraway land of Canaan.

As the caravan carrying their precious Rebekah headed out, the family prayed and blessed the daughter and sister they would probably never see again with these words—

Our sister, may you become the mother of thousands of ten thousands; and may your descendants possess the gates of those who hate them (Genesis 24:60).

If you are a mother, consider your impact. Your children are a blessing and a heritage from God, a source of joy to be brought up in the training and instruction of the Lord. When their time to leave home comes, you will be sad...but you can also rejoice in what their future holds. If they are willing, God will use them through the ages to affect thousands as they pass the baton of faith to yet another generation.

So your mission is clear. It's never too early to start your children's spiritual education. What are you doing today to train their hearts and minds and prepare them to leave a "legacy of faith" tomorrow?

The ABCs of Living God's Will

And [Rebekah] followed the man.
GENESIS 24:61

Knowing God's will is our greatest treasure. As you pray, seek godly counsel, and live according to what is revealed in God's Word, you'll discover His specific will for you. Learn more from the following ABCs based on God's will for Rebekah and how His will was revealed.

Ask God. Abraham's servant prayed fervently and specifically about finding the right wife for Isaac.

Ask God. Through prayer and by reading God's Word, you can access the heart and mind of the Lord.

Be faithful. Rebekah was led to the next phase of God's will for her life while she was faithfully serving her family in the details of daily life.

Be faithful. The need to make a decision is never a reason to neglect your duties. God leads you as you remain obedient in everyday life.

Consult others. Rebekah's father and brother were involved in counseling her and agreed to her marriage to Isaac.

Consult others. "Where there is no counsel, the people fall; but in the multitude of counselors there is safety" (Proverbs 11:14).

Decide for yourself. Family members agreed, God's will was evident, but Rebekah had to choose to follow God's plan.

Decide for yourself. You can be seeking, obedient, and asking, but ultimately you must decide to act on God's will.

Execute your decision. Rather than lingering, Rebekah acted immediately and began her journey of faith...by faith!

Execute your decision. Once you know God's will, take action! Move out. Go full speed ahead.

Ask God to open your eyes and your heart to His will for you. And don't be surprised when you discover it's right in front of you!

Following a Divine Design

She became his wife.

GENESIS 24:67

*W*hat a romantic and dramatic moment when Rebekah and her husband Isaac were at last united! After a long journey through the desert Rebekah finally caught her first glimpse of her husband-to-be. He was in the fields meditating. Can you picture him walking and praying and waiting? When he saw the caravan he probably wondered, *Can it be Eliezer? Did the old servant find a bride for me?* The answer was yes.

Isaac "took Rebekah and she became his wife, and he loved her."

Rebekah then took the next step in God's divine design for her. She endeavored to follow His instructions for a wife. What does that mean?

- *Leave your family and cleave to your husband.* When you marry, you're freed from the authority of your parents to be joyfully bound to your husband. He is now the most important person in your life (Genesis 2:24).

- *Help your husband.* God has ordained your role as assisting your husband with his responsibilities, his tasks, his goals (Genesis 2:18).

- *Follow your husband.* God has given the difficult role of leadership to your husband. Your role is to follow (Genesis 3:16; Ephesians 5:22).

- *Respect your husband.* How lovely to be in the presence of a wife who respects her husband. She treats him as she would respond to Christ. This is God's lovely, high calling for you (Ephesians 5:33).

How well are you following God's divine design? Do any areas need improvement?

Depending Fully on the Lord

She went to inquire of the Lord.

GENESIS 25:22

Rebekah was growing in the Lord. One of the lessons she learned was that prayer is the best way to handle difficulties. Two major blessings in her life happened when people prayed:

Abraham's servant prayed for a bride for Abraham's son Isaac—and God led him to Rebekah. Prayer was a key factor in Rebekah becoming Isaac's wife.

When Rebekah was barren after 20 years of marriage, Isaac prayed and Rebekah conceived. Prayer was the primary reason she was able to get pregnant.

But Rebekah had a "problem pregnancy." As the pregnancy and her worries continued, Rebekah's spiritual growth showed. She "went to inquire of the LORD." Her understanding of God's power encouraged her to depend on Him more fully. And she was not disappointed. The Lord spoke to her!

Like Rebekah, you can depend more fully on God's power and His love by praying during difficulties. Asking through prayer helps you see your problem in light of God's power. Asking in prayer reaps other fruit too:

- Prayer deepens your insight into what you really need.

- Prayer broadens your appreciation for God's answers.

- Prayer allows you to mature so you can use His gifts more wisely.[2]

What pains, trials, temptations, or sufferings are you facing today? Follow in Rebekah's footsteps of faith and take your concerns to the Lord. Set your heart on the Lord and depend fully on Him. Make prayer your first option.

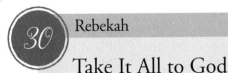

Take It All to God

The Lord said to her...
GENESIS 25:23

*E*veryone struggles. We struggle in marriage, with finances, with health problems, with family members, with career, with jobs, with friends, and with temptation. For the beautiful wife Rebekah, however, there was literally an internal struggle. Finally pregnant after 20 years of marriage to Isaac, she knew something was not right in her pregnancy. An extraordinary commotion raged inside and made her uneasy. So she went to the only Person who could help her—she prayed to the Lord. The answer to her prayer—and the relief for her struggle—was in God's hands. No one else could help.

First, only God could know Rebekah was carrying twins. God forms the inward parts of each child in the womb of its mother, and its frame is not hidden from Him (see Psalm 139:13-16). Rebekah's twins were the first recorded in Scripture.

Second, only God could know the futures of Rebekah's twin sons. He answered Rebekah's question, "Why am I like this?" with a prophecy regarding her twins: "Two nations are in your womb, two peoples shall be separated from your body; one people shall be stronger than the other, and the older shall serve the younger (Genesis 15:23)." Her twins would reverse the traditional roles—the older would serve the younger—and the two would struggle as each became a great nation.

When perplexed, disturbed, anxious, and distressed Rebekah responded by approaching God. Is this your practice too? Take your struggles and routinely...

- go into the sanctuary of God (Psalm 73:17),

- spread your case before the Lord (2 Kings 19:14), and

- ask counsel at the Almighty's throne (Hebrews 4:16).

T-R-U-S-T

> *She is my sister.*
> GENESIS 26:7

Rebekah, a daughter, a wife, and a mother, had successfully weathered a series of significant faith ventures.

- *Separation*—Rebekah left family and home to marry Isaac, heir to God's promise to make Abraham's descendants into a great nation.

- *Marriage*—Rebekah made the necessary adjustments to married life and her marriage partner.

- *Childlessness*—Two decades passed as Rebekah and Isaac waited for a child.

- *Motherhood*—Finally two babies were born. Being the mother of the world's first-recorded twins surely stretched Rebekah's faith.

But Rebekah's beauty endured...and presented another test of faith. There was a famine, but God instructed Isaac to stay put. Because he was afraid the Philistines would kill him and take his beautiful wife, Isaac told the king, "She is my sister."

What would you have done? If you're frozen with fear,

Trust in God—not your husband (1 Peter 3:1-2).

Refuse to succumb to fear (1 Peter 3:6).

Understand God always watches over you (Psalm 23:4).

Strengthen your spirit with God's promises (2 Peter 1:4).

Thank God for His promised protection (Isaiah 41:10).

To better understand what it means to trust God, look up each verse listed with T-R-U-S-T. Ask God to help you rely on Him when you are tested.

Trust in God's Love and Leading

God Is Always Working

Rachel came with her father's sheep.
GENESIS 29:9

Experts on proper etiquette tell us to include personal information when we introduce someone. In Genesis 29:9, God introduces us to another amazing single woman named Rachel. Note her personal information.

- *Her family*—Rachel was the daughter of Laban, Rebekah's brother, and therefore in the line of Abraham.

- *Her occupation*—Rachel was a shepherdess. In fact, the name Rachel means "ewe."

- *Her appearance*—"Rachel was beautiful of form and appearance." Like her Aunt Rebekah, she was lovely to look at.

God also introduces us to Jacob, a person important to Him...and who will soon be important to Rachel.

- *His family*—Jacob and his twin brother, Esau, were

the sons of Isaac and Rebekah, who came from Rachel's homeland. Jacob and his brother were also grandsons of Abraham.

- *His predicament*—Favoritism, jealousy, and deceit led Jacob to flee to Rachel's homeland to escape being murdered by Esau. Furthermore, Isaac advised Jacob to find a wife from among his own people (Genesis 28:2).

God brought Rachel and Jacob together by working through *people, events,* and *circumstances*, and the same is true for you. Look back over the last few days and weeks. How did God work through people, events, and circumstances to bring about good for you? Some happenings may not seem good in this lifetime, but you can trust a loving God that there is and will be good!

Trust in Ordinary Wonder

Rachel came with her father's sheep.
GENESIS 29:9

The day began like every other day. As the younger woman Rachel mentally ran through her list of chores, she saw no hint that today her life would be dramatically transformed. At the top of Rachel's to-do list was one very necessary responsibility: "Water father's sheep." As she approached the well that afternoon, Rachel noticed a stranger. He stood with other shepherds talking and presumably waiting for a larger group to gather before rolling the stone away from the well's mouth so the sheep could drink. Rachel was surprised when the handsome stranger ran to the well, lifted off the rock, and began watering her sheep. Then he kissed her, wept, and explained they were relatives.

That was the beginning of the courtship of Rachel and Jacob. Rachel's ordinary day became extraordinary.

How does a single woman meet the man of her dreams? Here are two keys from Rachel's experience:

Rachel was busy. She was where she was supposed to be (at the town well) and doing what she was supposed to be doing (watering her father's sheep).

Rachel was faithful. Tending and watering her father's sheep were Rachel's responsibilities. As she faithfully discharged her duty, God was leading her to her destiny.

If you are single and looking for a marriage partner, don't be in a hurry. Don't look for miracles. Don't look for the extraordinary. Continue in your usual manner and trust God's leading. He often reveals His divine plans in small, ordinary events.

"Don't look for miracles" also applies to married women. Pray for your husband, but don't wait for him to change. Please God by being the best wife you can be.

A Woman After God's Own Heart

Leah's eyes were delicate.
GENESIS 29:17

Your beauty should not come from outward adornment, such as braided hair and the wearing of gold jewelry and fine clothes. Instead, it should be that of your inner self, the unfading beauty of a gentle and quiet spirit, which is of great worth in God's sight" (1 Peter 3:3-4 NIV). These few verses give us God's standards for beauty. Take to heart His beauty tips!

Nurture the beauty of your heart. God values godly character, which shines in positive, outward conduct. Fashion your heart after Jesus.

Cultivate the beauty of a gentle and quiet spirit. God treasures the soft graces of a calm, quiet spirit—not costly clothes and jewels. Focus on what's inside.

Concern yourself with inner beauty, which is precious in the sight of God. Your supreme goal in life is to be pleasing in His sight. Fix your eyes on Him.

Leah, Rachel's sister, was destined to live her life in the shadow of Rachel's exquisite beauty. Not only was Leah—whose name means "wearied" or "faint from sickness"—less than beautiful, but her eyes were delicate, weak, and dull—a serious blemish at the time. But even great beauty fades.

Aren't you glad God is more concerned about inner beauty? Aren't you thankful "the Lord does not see as man sees; for man looks at the outward appearance, but the Lord looks at the heart" (1 Samuel 16:7)?

Tend to your inner beauty by spending time each day in the presence of the Lord, discovering more about Him and how you can better please Him. He will transform you into a woman of true beauty...a woman after His heart.

35 Leah

Turning Ashes to Beauty

He took Leah...and brought her to Jacob.
GENESIS 29:33

*L*eah's father, Laban, was a master of deception. Because of her own father, Leah was used, mistreated, and rejected.

- Jacob, a distant cousin to Leah and Rachel, came to their home to seek a bride.

- Rachel, Leah's beautiful sister, met Jacob at the city well, and the two instantly fell in love.

- Laban, Rachel's father, contracted with Jacob for seven years of indentured service in exchange for Rachel's hand in marriage. On the wedding night, however, Laban secretly substituted Leah for Rachel.

- The result? Leah was used by her father, unloved by her husband, and envied by her sister (Genesis 30:1).

Disappointment is a fact of life. Have you been unfairly used? Deceived? Rejected? Let God's love comfort you. Leah was not beautiful—and neither were her circumstances.

But God exchanged her sorrow for blessings. What emerged from Leah's trials and disappointment?

- With her imperfect eyes, she may have never married, yet she had a husband.
- She may never have had children, yet she had six boys and one girl.
- She was the mother of 6 of the men who led the 12 tribes of Israel.
- She was the mother of Judah, through whom Jesus Christ would come.
- She was the first or "recognized" wife of Jacob.

Leah

Proof of God's Love

The LORD has surely looked on my affliction.

GENESIS 29:32

What's in a name? Plenty! In Bible times, names given to newborns were very significant. A name expressed the parents' feelings and many times alluded to circumstances in the family's history. Often the relationship the parents enjoyed with God was evident in their baby's name. Through the names they bestowed, mothers and fathers passed on their expectations, their faith, and a bit of their hard-earned wisdom. Such is the case of Leah. As you follow Leah on her journey, you'll see that the names of her children mark her spiritual growth. Here's what happened.

The lackluster Leah had the misfortune of sharing her husband, Jacob, with her stunning sister, Rachel. The Bible tells us Jacob loved Rachel more than Leah and that Leah was unloved. Both Leah and Rachel were barren for a while, but the Lord eventually opened Leah's womb, and she conceived and bore a son.

When she held her new baby, Leah christened him "Reuben"—"See, a son!" or "Behold a son!" Leah exclaimed, "The LORD has surely looked on my affliction. Now therefore, my husband will love me (Genesis 29:32)." The name "Reuben" reveals Leah's longing for love. She hoped Jacob would turn his heart toward her as he held his first child.

But buried deeper in the naming of her tiny boy was her joyful surprise at God's love and compassion. "Reuben" also acknowledges God's kindness and providence. He'd noticed her trouble and looked favorably upon Leah. She treasured that thought so deeply that it was passed on to her son. To Leah, Reuben would always be proof of God's loving care.

Lord, thank You for the proof of Your love for me that came with Jesus' death on the cross. Help me remember that any momentary affliction is a small price to pay for the hope of the life to come I have in Jesus. Amen.

Leah

Your Vibrant Rainbow

Now I will praise the LORD.
GENESIS 29:35

Everyone experiences disappointment and lack, loss and sorrow. Everyone has thwarted dreams and hopes. Everyone contends with problems and conflicts. Whatever clouds and storms you've encountered, your victory over them stands as a brilliant rainbow of God's grace.

Leah, the wife of Jacob, lived a life ravaged by hardship. Yet she enjoyed such a brilliant victory in her problem-filled life. Locked in a loveless marriage, Leah also shared her husband with her younger, more beautiful sister. Yet Leah was the wife God blessed with bearing most of Jacob's children.

Child #1 was named Reuben.

Child #2 was christened Simeon.

Child #3 was called Levi.

And then came the fourth child—"Judah," meaning "praise." The arc of the rainbow was clear and complete as praise rang through Leah's tent. "Now I will praise the LORD!" she exclaimed.

What made the rainbow complete was Leah's apparent submission to the Lord and her victory over her circumstances. Leah finally ceased fretting about the absence of Jacob's love and instead rested in God's love. In Him she found joy and multiple reasons to praise. And through Judah the Messiah would come! Every generation would know who Leah's fourth son was.

You can follow Leah's path to victory. Praise your all-wise, ever-loving, forever-faithful Father...even through tears and in dark times. Trust in God's leading. Rest in His love and offer Him praise that fills in the vivid, joyful colors of the rich rainbow of His grace to you.

38

Leah

Nurturing Strong Roots

Now I will praise the LORD.

GENESIS 29:35

Whatat does it take to become strong in the Lord? What can you glean from the following story?

In bygone days there was a process used for growing the trees that became the main masts for military and merchant ships. The great shipbuilders first selected a tree located on the top of a high hill as a potential mast. Then they cut away all of the surrounding trees that would shield the chosen one from the force of the wind. As the years went by and the winds blew fiercely against the tree, the tree only grew stronger until finally it was strong enough to be the foremast of a ship. [3]

Fierce winds blew in Leah's life. Her father's mistreatment, her husband's hatred, and her sister's envy hurled against her. But Leah deepened her faith and received from God what she needed. She shouted, "Now I will praise the LORD!"

Stand up in the place where the dear Lord has put you, and there do your best. God gives us trials and tests. Out of the buffeting of a serious conflict we are expected to grow strong. The tree that grows where tempests toss its boughs and bend its trunk often almost to breaking, is often more firmly rooted than the tree which grows in the sequestered valley where no storm ever brings stress or strain. The same is true of life.[4]

Buffeting, conflicts, tempests, storms, stresses, strains—all are God's prods to help you attain greater faith and strength.

39

Bilhah

Might from Meekness

And [Rachel] gave him Bilhah her maid.
GENESIS 30:4

Jesus taught, "Blessed are the meek, for they shall inherit the earth." Paul wrote, "When I am weak, then I am strong." Hannah prayed, "The LORD...brings low and lifts up."* Do you see the common theme? In God's world, "might" comes from "meekness." If you find yourself in a lowly position, or if you are struggling under oppression, or if you're living in a God-ordained season in the shade, take heart!

Sentenced to a life of slavery, the woman Bilhah had little to look forward to. Her life wasn't her own. In fact, she was passed from person to person and was given to Rachel by her master when Rachel married Jacob. Yet Bilhah discovered God's blessings in the midst of her lowly existence.

Bilhah couldn't help but notice the domestic tensions in her new home. Jacob's two wives, Leah and Rachel, were

---

* Matthew 5:5, 2 Corinthians 12:10, 1 Samuel 2:7

constantly at odds. Jacob clearly loved Rachel more than he did Leah. And Leah gave birth to son after son, while the barren Rachel burned with envy.

During a heated argument with her husband, Rachel announced, "Here is my maid Bilhah; go in to her, and she will bear a child on my knees, that I also may have children by her." Bilhah had been given away again! But this time from meekness would arise might...through Bilhah's offspring.

Dan was Bilhah's firstborn by Jacob. From Dan sprang the mighty Samson, the renowned judge and deliverer of Israel, whose exceptional physical strength was greatly used by God. Naphtali was Bilhah's second son by Jacob. He too grew strong and became the founder of a large tribe of people.

This servant was blessed by God with two sons who inherited a portion of Jacob's vast wealth and became powerful leaders of two of the twelve tribes of Israel!

Lessons in the Waiting

God remembered Rachel, and God listened to her.

GENESIS 30:22

econd only to suffering, waiting may be the greatest teacher and trainer in godliness, maturity, and genuine spirituality most of us ever encounter."[5] Rachel definitely put in her time of waiting! Her expectation that she would one day be a mother grew out of God's promise to her husband's grandfather Abraham that his seed would become a great nation equaling in number the stars in the sky and the grains of sand on the seashores (Genesis 12:2-3; 22:17). Yet Rachel and Jacob waited...and waited...and waited.

How long did Rachel wait? It probably seemed like forever. She waited while 10 children were born to Jacob by her sister, Leah, and two servants named Bilhah and Zilpah. It's possible that a quarter of a century passed while Rachel remained childless.

What spiritual lessons did she learn? And how can what she learned help you in your faith journey?

The lesson of prayer. Rachel discovered the power of prayer. Genesis 30:22 says, "And God listened to her and opened her womb." Prayer will still your fretting heart as you look to God for what is lacking in your life. Prayer also sculpts your heart into the beautiful posture of humility.

The lesson of faith. In naming her long-desired son, Rachel exhibited extraordinary faith. "She called his name Joseph [meaning "God will add"] and said, 'The Lord shall add to me another son.'" Rachel's faith—enshrined in the name of her son—reached out and pressed on for more than God had yet given.

How patient are you? Are you waiting for healing? Are you waiting for reconciliation, renewal, or revival? What are you learning as you wait? And what blessings are you reaching for by faith? Pray faithfully as you wait on the Lord. Be assured that He is leading you to His good and acceptable and perfect will.

Rachel and Leah

Stepping into the Unknown

Whatever God has said to you, do it.
GENESIS 31:16

From the beginning of time God gave a divine principle for marriage: "Therefore a man shall leave his father and mother and be joined to his wife, and they shall become one flesh" (Genesis 2:24).

After running away from Esau, Jacob spent many years with relatives. Finally he wanted to return home. Detailing God's leading and pointing to His hand of blessing, Jacob asked his two wives, Rachel and Leah, to go with him. He wanted to take a willing family on his pilgrimage home...a family filled with faith. Would Rachel and Leah stay in their father's familiar house or go with their husband to a foreign land?

Leaving and cleaving is always a test of faith for a wife.

- It tests her obedience to God's Word and His way.

- It tests her faith in God's leading through a husband.

- It tests her trust in her husband's wisdom.

- It tests her commitment to her husband.

How did Rachel and Leah answer Jacob? "Whatever God has said to you, do it." What amazing faith and support! As they stepped out and followed God, they joined God's other women of faith.

Are you a wife? Is your husband Number One in your life (after God)? Is there stress and conflict surrounding your marriage and your parents? Consider signing an agreement that spells out your status as a wife. The wording might be: "I am no longer accountable to my parents. I am free from that authority and now bound joyfully and securely to my mate."[6]

Are you a mother of married children? If so, consider signing such a statement that releases them to follow God's leading with their mates.

Loving Is Serving

Deborah, Rebekah's nurse, died.
GENESIS 35:8

As Rebekah's faithful nursemaid, Deborah made the arduous 500-mile trip from Haran to Hebron when Rebekah went to marry Abraham's son Isaac. There Deborah also weathered Rebekah's ups and downs during her 20 years of waiting for a child. When Rebekah's twin boys finally arrived, Deborah lovingly and tenderly cared for Jacob and Esau.

Age brought an end to Deborah's active role of caregiver, and then Jacob's family cared for her. She loved them, and they loved her. After approximately 100 years of life, Deborah was buried under "the oak of weeping" and was lamented with sadness and tears usually reserved for family.

Deborah is a beautiful portrait of devoted service. As a representative of God, you too are called to love all with God's love. The ultimate expression of love is service freely and abundantly given. Take to heart these truths...

Love bears all things,

Love believes all things,
Love hopes all things,
Love endures all things,
Love never fails. [7]

Servanthood is a hallmark of the Christian faith. What can you do today to demonstrate your heart of love and service? Who needs your help? Your care?

Rachel

Ministering God's Love

You will have this son also.

GENESIS 35:17

*R*achel, wife of Jacob, died in childbirth. She was buried near Bethlehem, and her grave was marked by a pillar raised in her memory by her devoted husband. She was survived by Jacob, her sister Leah, her firstborn son Joseph, and her new baby Benjamin.

Rachel's death offers us two fascinating firsts.

- Rachel's death is the first instance of death during childbirth recorded in the Bible. Journeying from Bethel to Ephrath, Rachel "labored in childbirth, and she had hard labor." In an effort to encourage and comfort the distraught Rachel, her midwife said, "Do not fear; you will have this son also." Her words came true, but the beginning of Rachel's second son's life marked the end of her own.

- The pillar the grieving Jacob set up on Rachel's grave is the first grave marker on record in the Bible.

Rachel's life was marked by great love and marred by many struggles. Two phrases could have been engraved on the pillar erected in her honor:

- *A loved wife.* Rachel was Jacob's true love from the moment they met.

- *A loving mother.* At one time Rachel demanded of Jacob, "Give me children, or else I die" (Genesis 30:1). Eventually God blessed Rachel, and she poured love into her son Joseph, who grew up and became the godliest and greatest of the 12 sons of Jacob.

Rachel's chief contribution to God's kingdom happened in her home and in the hearts of those nearest and dearest to her. Like Rachel, major on ministering God's love at home and to those around you.

Forging Ahead with Faith

There I buried Leah.

GENESIS 49:31

*W*e don't know how Leah's life ended. The only mention of her death is when Jacob said, "I buried Leah."

Leah's life was filled with pain and sorrow, discouragement and disappointment, setbacks and letdowns. Yet even as she lived her life in the shadow of Jacob and Rachel's bright love, she enjoyed three tremendous blessings as she forged ahead.

- Leah was blessed by God with six sons and one daughter. One of her sons was Judah, through whose line the Savior Jesus Christ would come.

- Leah was buried with her husband. Leah, not Rachel, lay next to Jacob in the family tomb.

- Leah is listed in God's *Who's Who* (Genesis 49:31). Leah (meaning "weak" and "faint") is among those forever remembered, along with Abraham, Isaac, and Jacob, and their wives, Sarah and Rebekah.

Every life—including yours—has its shadowlands. How can you move on through heartache? Follow what Leah learned—

Lesson #1: Take a long-range view. God's purposes are achieved through the whole of your life, not in fragments of a moment, a day, or a year. What counts most is the sum of your contributions. Being a devoted wife, a loving mother, and a benefit to those around you are contributions to God's kingdom that can never be fully measured.

Lesson #2: Give your love generously to as many as you can. It's not what you get, but what you give that is God's true measure of a life.

Trusting God's Outcome

There I buried Leah.

GENESIS 49:31

Far better than reading a volume of *Who's Who in Church History* is reading the Who's Who lists of men and women who shaped the nation of Israel. One such list appears in Genesis 49. Leah is included in this roll call of very important people, which shows us something very important about who matters in the kingdom of God.

As Jacob, the son of Isaac and grandson of Abraham, lay dying in Egypt, he first blessed his 12 sons. Then, having pronounced his blessings, Jacob charged his sons to bury him in the field of Machpelah in the land of Canaan and explained why:

> There they buried Abraham and Sarah his wife,
> there they buried Isaac and Rebekah his wife,
> and there I buried Leah.

At long last Leah is honored by her husband. During Leah's life Jacob never pretended to love her and never hid his love for her sister, Rachel. But in the end he requested to be buried alongside Leah. And Leah—not Rachel—is listed in the Who's Who of patriarchal couples through whom God extended the promise of a Savior. Leah is mentioned right beside Abraham, Isaac, Jacob, Sarah, and Rebekah. Faithful Leah finally received the honor she never knew during her days on earth.

Your calling—like Leah's—is to remain faithful...to the end. Honor is not always bestowed along life's way. Flowers may be thrown across your path, but the winner's wreath is not awarded until the end of the contest. Regardless of obstacles en route to glory, regardless of sorrow or mistreatment on your journey to paradise, look only to the Lord. He is standing at the end to receive you...at the end to reward you. Wait for God's "well done." It will come!

Courage to Rise to the Challenge

Shiprah and Puah

Choose God's Way

You shall kill him.

EXODUS 1:16

Every problem requires a solution, and the Pharaoh of Egypt had a big one—Joseph, the son of Rachel and Jacob. During a devastating famine the only food available was in Egypt, so Jacob and his family moved there. They were reunited with Joseph and enjoyed many wonderful years together until "there arose a new king over Egypt, who did not know Joseph. And he said to his people, 'Look, the people of the children of Israel are more and mightier than we'" (Exodus 1:8-9).

- *The problem*—The rapid increase in the number of Israelites.
- *The solution*—Murder every male baby.
- *The means*—The Hebrew midwives Shiprah and Puah.

Shiprah and Puah were professionals who assisted Hebrew women with childbirth and the initial care of their newborns. When these two women were commanded to kill the babies they were helping bring into the world, they faced a huge dilemma.

- *The problem*—They were ordered to kill every male baby born to the Hebrews.
- *The solution*—Because they feared God, the women quietly disobeyed the order.

Every problem tests the mettle of your allegiance to God and His standards. Every problem says, "Whom will you obey?" Take courage from Shiphrah and Puah, who risked their lives by disregarding Pharaoh's command to kill. Be bold every time a problem comes up and choose God's way.

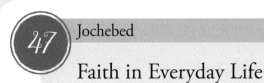

47 Jochebed

Faith in Everyday Life

She hid [her baby] three months.

EXODUS 2:2

Have you wondered what true faith looks like in everyday life? Meet Jochebed, a true picture of faith in action and note a few key facts about this great woman of faith.

Her heritage. A daughter of Levi, Jochebed married Amram, a man of the house of Levi (Exodus 2:1; 6:20). Through Levi, Jochebed and Amram inherited the faith of Abraham, Isaac, and Jacob.

Her situation. As the mother of a newborn boy, Jochebed faced a frightening dilemma. She knew the Egyptian Pharaoh had ordered every son born of the Jews to be cast into the Nile River to die (Exodus 1:22).

Her faith. Motivated by her trust in God and her love for her child, Jochebed took a bold step of faith and hid little Moses. This singular act of faith qualified her as one whose life testifies of faith in God. Only three women—Sarah, Rahab, and Jochebed—are noted among God's heroes of faith (Hebrews 11). Of Jochebed Scripture says, "By faith Moses, when he was born, was hidden three months by his parents, because...they were not afraid of the king's command" (verse 23).

Her decision. Jochebed's faith fueled her courage. Deciding to neither obey Pharaoh's command nor fear him or any consequences, she trusted God and kept her baby alive.

How does your faith show in your everyday life? What acts or choices might people notice that reveal your love and obedience for Him? As a child of God, hold up your frightening, seemingly impossible situations to your Father in heaven. Realize that worry ends when faith begins...and that faith ends when worry begins. Declare with David, "Whenever I am afraid, I will trust in You" (Psalm 56:3).

Take the Risk!

She took an ark...and laid it...by the river's bank.

<small>EXODUS 2:3</small>

The wise writer of Ecclesiastes tells women who love God to "cast your bread upon the waters, for you will find it after many days" (11:1). This principle for living a life of faith alludes to the agricultural practice of throwing seed upon water or soggy ground and then waiting for it to produce a harvest. Like a farmer, at times you must take a risk in order to enjoy the rewards of faith. You must step out *before* you can receive God's blessing.

When the Egyptian Pharaoh ordered every male baby born to the Jews to be drowned in the Nile, Jochebed was forced to take a chance with her "seed"...with her tiny baby, Moses. She hid her little babe for three months. Then, realizing she could no longer conceal a vigorous infant and trusting God, Jochebed "took an ark of bulrushes...put the child in it, and laid it in the reeds by the river's bank." She was casting her bread—her beloved son—upon the waters.

In His great providence, God brought Pharaoh's

daughter to the riverbank. She found the ark and had compassion for the infant. Needing a nursemaid for the baby, the princess found Jochebed—further evidence of God's providence. Jochebed was allowed to keep and nurse the precious babe she'd placed into the hands of God by putting him into the river. Jochebed's seed of faith sprouted!

What challenge in your life requires a risk of faith? Are you sending your child off to school or college, off to a new married life, off to a job in another city or state, off to serve God on the mission field or in the military? Do you feel you're losing him or her? Have the faith of Jochebed. Be courageous. Take the risk and let go. Trust God that you will eventually reap His blessings.

A Brave Heart

The daughter of Pharaoh...had compassion on him.

Exodus 2:5-6

*T*wo things stand like stone:

> Kindness in another's troubles;
> Courage in one's own. [8]

Little is known about the mysterious daughter of Pharaoh, but her kindness and courage have endured through the ages. The Scriptures tell of that sunny day when this princess approached the Nile River for her bath. While wading along the river's edge, she caught sight of a floating basket, which she discovered held a small baby boy. This woman knew the baby was one of the Hebrews' children her father had ordered killed, but she had compassion for him. The Pharaoh's daughter had a very big—and brave—heart!

- *She was compassionate.* Hearing the baby's cries, the

daughter of the powerful Pharaoh drew the infant out of the water and named him Moses.

- *She was kind.* At the risk of jeopardizing her relationship with her father, this princess thought it too cruel to murder the little infant she held. She offered kindness to someone in trouble.

- *She was courageous.* Compassion and kindness kindled courage in the princess and overshadowed any fear she had of disobeying her father.

Although Pharaoh's daughter was a pagan, God used her kindness and courage to benefit His people. This tender woman of the past—whose name we don't even know—challenges us today. Pray to be more kind to others in distress. To be courageous and compassionate when the need arises.

Clever and Gutsy Miriam

So [Miriam] went and called the child's mother.

EXODUS 2:8

Traditionally Jewish girls remained under the guidance of their mothers until marriage. So by the time Moses was born, Miriam had been taught the valuable qualities of diligence, faithfulness, responsibility, and wisdom by Jochebed. The young Miriam clearly exhibited each of these virtues.

Since Pharaoh had commanded that every Hebrew boy be drowned, when Moses' parents gave birth to a little boy, they hid him until he could no longer be kept quiet. The distressful day came when they placed Moses in a basket on the river. Even though they knew God would watch over him, it was still heartbreaking.

Perhaps Moses' mother couldn't bear to watch what might happen to her dear baby. Or perhaps her presence at the riverbank would've been too obvious. Or did she ask Miriam to stand nearby and watch over the basket? Or did the spunky, devoted sister decide on her own to stay and look out for her baby brother? However it happened, she was there when Pharaoh's daughter came to bathe and ended up rescuing the infant. Thinking fast, the clever and gutsy Miriam stepped forward and asked, "Shall I go and call a nurse for you from the Hebrew women, that she may nurse the child for you?" Given permission by the princess, Miriam brought Jochebed to feed him! Because of Miriam's love for her infant brother and her quick thinking, a double blessing was reaped by her family.

- Jochebed received her baby back.
- Jochebed received wages for nursing Moses.

Teaching your little ones about love, mercy, caring, and compassion, along with diligence, faithfulness, responsibility, and wisdom—the kinds of traits we see in Miriam—begins with you. They will grow up to mirror your merits. What are they seeing in you and learning from your actions?

Making Each Day Count

[Jochebed] took the child and nursed him.
EXODUS 2:9

God gives Christian parents the assignment of training up children for Him. Proverbs 22:6 says, "Train up a child in the way he should go." Jochebed raised Moses, her youngest child, for his first three years and then had to turn him over to his adoptive mom. Can you imagine how much her heart hurt when she had to give Moses to Pharaoh's daughter to raise? But Jochebed's faithful everyday training during those three years bore fruit in her son's life. The second half of Proverbs 22:6 came true, "When he is old he will not depart from it." At age 40 Moses chose to identify with God's people rather than remain in Pharaoh's palace (Hebrews 11:24-26). That was his first giant step toward the important role God had for him.

Deuteronomy 6:5-7 gives us two guidelines for training children:

Love God. "You shall love the LORD your God with all your heart, with all your soul, and with all your strength." Devote yourself to your heavenly Father. Love Him more than anyone or anything else.

Teach God's Word. "You shall teach [My words] diligently to your children and shall talk of them when you sit in your house, when you walk by the way, when you lie down, and when you rise up." Faithfully communicate the truths of Scripture.

An axiom of teaching warns, "You cannot impart what you do not possess." Is God the focus of your life? Is pleasing Him the overarching concern of your life? With a foundation of deep love for God and His Word hidden in your heart, you definitely have something crucial to share with your children. Consciously and constantly make each day count—talk to your children about God.

Jochebed

Empowered Against Evil

She brought [Moses] to Pharaoh's daughter.

EXODUS 2:10

All around you is evidence that evil is in this fallen world. Terrible news comes in from all over the world. But take heart! You can make a difference. Take the mother Jochebed, for instance. She lived in an evil world that was growing darker every day. When her third baby was born, the Egyptian Pharaoh put forth his evil hand of oppression. He ordered that every boy born to the Jews be murdered (Exodus 1:16,22). What could Jochebed—a godly woman and devoted mother—do against such evil? She could take action in faith!

- *Courage*—Jochebed decided to keep her baby rather than kill him, thereby preserving him to bless the world.

- *Creativity*—Jochebed made a basket from bulrushes, covered it with tar and mud for waterproofing, and then put her baby in it so he would float in the

Nile River close to where Pharaoh's daughter came regularly.

- *Care*—During the brief time she had Moses, Jochebed lovingly nursed and diligently trained him in the ways of the Lord.

- *Confidence*—After giving her son loving care and spiritual instruction, Jochebed returned her son to Pharaoh's household, trusting God would care for her boy.

God used Jochebed's courage, creativity, care, and confidence in God to position her son inside the house of Pharaoh. There he was educated and became familiar with Egyptian ways and God later used Moses to deliver His people from oppression.

If you're a mom, don't fret because of evildoers. Instead take up the challenge and devote yourself to raising children who love God. And take heart! The prince of darkness is helpless against the power of the truth you plant in your children's hearts and minds.

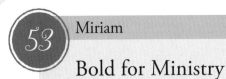
Bold for Ministry

Miriam...the sister of [Moses and] Aaron...
Exodus 15:20

*M*iriam, what advice do you have for single women?"
Imagine an interviewer today asking this question of Miriam, one of God's super-singles of yesterday.

Perhaps Miriam would simply say, "Devote yourself to ministry." Based on the Bible, Miriam appears to have viewed her singleness as an opportunity to give herself fully to ministry. As a result she blossomed into one of the Bible's strongest female leaders (Micah 6:4). Throughout the deliverance of God's people from Egyptian bondage and their journey into the Promised Land, Miriam accompanied and assisted her brothers, Aaron and Moses, in their leadership of the Israelites.

If you're unmarried, join Miriam in her view of ministry. Yes, you may have your career (that is also an important opportunity for ministry), but the rest of your time is available.

Whether you're single or married, take time to pray about these two questions:

How effectively am I using my "free" time—my evenings, my weekends, my children's naptimes—for God's kingdom?

What doors of ministry are open to me now?

Just think of the myriad of ministries you could have during your free time. You could mentor another woman. You could write or email a lonely missionary. You could take a special meal to a person suffering physically. You could visit a shut-in. You could help your church prepare for worship services. Rise to the challenge and take a bold step into the realm of selfless ministry. Make time for it.

Praising and Prophesying

Miriam, the prophetess...
EXODUS 15:20

A prophetess received messages from God and shared them with others. She openly praised the Lord with words and songs that come from or were inspired by Him. Only a handful of women in Scripture were given this role and title. They include Miriam, Deborah, Huldah, Anna, and Philip's four daughters.[9] Miriam is the first woman noted in Scripture with this rare honor.

The years before Miriam's prophesying included her people's bondage under the oppressive hand of the Egyptians. When the sons of Israel cried out to God for help, God sent Moses and Aaron, Miriam's brothers, to negotiate the Israelites' freedom. Times were tense because Pharaoh increased the Jews' workload and repeatedly changed his mind about their release. After ten encounters with Moses and numerous plagues choreographed by God, including the death of all the firstborn Egyptian children and livestock, Pharaoh finally allowed the Israelites to leave. But even then he was so angry he soon sent an army in pursuit (Exodus 14:7).

This dramatic situation was the backdrop for one more mighty and supernatural act. As soon as the Jewish people walked through the miraculously parted Red Sea waters, God just as miraculously closed the waters, drowning the entire Egyptian army. What wonder! What relief for the Jews! What deliverance!

Moses immediately erupted into a song of praise, and Miriam also offered her own God-inspired song of praise. With tambourine in hand and followed by all the women dancing and playing their tambourines, Miriam exulted, "Sing to the LORD, for He has triumphed gloriously! The horse and its rider He has thrown into the sea!" Amen!

55 Miriam

Inspired to Serve

All the women went out after her.
EXODUS 15:20

*D*o you have aspirations for leadership? Consider a few principles of spiritual leadership. Then ask God to help develop them in you.

- *A leader is a follower.* To be a good leader you must first be a follower. Leadership is a discipline, and in the process of being a faithful follower you gain discipline.

- *A leader is a pray-er.* Prayer brings to leadership the power and energy of the Holy Spirit. Missionary and leader Hudson Taylor was convinced that it is possible to move others, through God, by prayer alone.

- *A leader is an initiator.* Authentic leaders take risks and move out courageously to make their vision happen.[10]

If you want a great model for leading—look at these same principles lived out in Miriam.

- *Miriam was a follower.* She faithfully served and assisted her brothers, Aaron and Moses, as they led God's people (Micah 6:4).

- *Miriam was a pray-er.* As a prophetess and woman of prayer, Miriam was filled with the Holy Spirit, who inspired her words.

- *Miriam was an initiator.* Moved by God's miraculous defeat of the Egyptian army in the midst of the Red Sea, Miriam "took the timbrel in her hand" and led the women in a song and dance of joy.

May God's Spirit and Miriam's example inspire you to serve the Lord and His people.

Nazirite Women

Set Apart for God

The vow of a Nazirite...

NUMBERS 6:2

As a believer in Jesus Christ, you are set apart to God. You have been delivered from the power of darkness and translated into the kingdom of God's Son (Colossians 1:13). Jesus accomplished these wonders for you.

In the time of Moses, a group of women chose to go beyond giving material possessions and time. God allowed for a special heart offering—a vow—for those laypeople who wanted to dedicate even more to Him. The law stated that when either a man or woman takes the vow of a Nazirite to separate himself to the Lord, he shall separate himself from certain items and practices.

What did a woman who took a voluntary Nazirite vow avoid? God's unusual list included wine, grape products, haircuts, and touching dead bodies. By submitting to these restrictions in their daily lives, those people who took the vow visibly and publicly set themselves apart from the world and declared their dedication to God.

How about you?

- Are you set apart to God in your heart and in your practices?

- Can others tell by your behavior, words, and attitudes that you are set apart from the world?

- Do people sense an otherworldliness about you...a wholehearted dedication to God?

- Have you set your affections on things above? Is your heart seeking those things that are of value to Christ (Colossians 3:1-2)?

Today dedicate yourself afresh to the Lord. Set yourself apart for God.

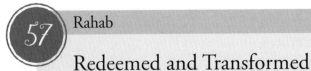

Redeemed and Transformed

[They] came to the house of a harlot named Rahab.

JOSHUA 2:1

"Rahab-the-harlot." Throughout the Bible, these three words refer to a remarkable woman who appears in faith's Hall of Fame (Hebrews 11). And she's got a before-and-after story to tell.

Before—Rahab was an idolatrous Amorite. Ra was the name of an Egyptian god, and Rahab's full name meant "insolent and fierce." The Bible also reports that Rahab was a harlot, a prostitute.

God's intervention—God touched Rahab's heart and transformed her into a new creature. For Rahab, old things passed away, and all things became new (2 Corinthians 5:17).

After—After her many heroic acts of faith, God abundantly blessed Rahab's life. What were some of the tangible blessings she received?

- Rahab married Salmon, a prince in the house of Judah.

- Rahab bore Salmon a son named Boaz...whose son was Obed...whose son was Jesse...whose son was David...through whose line Jesus was born (Ruth 4:20-22; Matthew 1:1 and 5).

Thank God for your own story of redemption and transformation. To the praise of the glory of His grace, God accepts you, redeems you, and forgives your sins (Ephesians 1:6-7).

An Astonishing Faith

For the LORD your God, He is God.
JOSHUA 2:11

*A*re you able to state clearly what you believe? Rahab did—and her statement of faith saved her life. Here's what happened.

The time came for God's people to enter the land God had promised them. Joshua, God's appointed leader, sent two of his warriors to check out the walled city of Jericho. While there, they lodged at Rahab's house. When the king of Jericho demanded Rahab hand over the men, Rahab acted with courage and quickly hid them and told the authorities they had already left.

Why did this harlot and resident of a godless town take such a risk? Hear Rahab's words to the spies...and her heart of faith in Joshua 2:9-11.

- I know that the LORD has given you the land.

- We have heard how the LORD dried up the water of the Red Sea for you when you came out of Egypt.

- The LORD your God, He is God in heaven above and on earth beneath.

Rahab's statement of faith clearly reveals her astonishing faith and knowledge of God. She obviously knew who God was and what He had done for His people. She knew of His plan to give the land to His chosen race. And she knew He was the God of all heaven and earth. Rahab definitely had her facts about God straight.

Take time to think...and pray...and articulate your beliefs. Search the Scriptures too. How would your statement of faith read? How much do you know about God and His dealings with His people? How many of His attributes are you familiar with? Know what you believe...and then, as Rahab did, declare your faith to others.

Boldly Asking and Acting

Give me also springs of water.
JOSHUA 15:19

$\mathcal{A}$chsah was a woman of courage and wisdom. The daughter of Caleb, a warrior who served Joshua, Achsah learned from her father to ask for what she wanted.

When Achsah married, the dowry Caleb gave included a portion of his land. Because water was critical in that arid climate, Achsah boldly said to her father, "Give me also springs of water." Like father, like daughter!

Achsah could be easily overlooked, but her life holds important messages.

Message #1: Watch. The wise woman "watches over the ways of her household" (Proverbs 31:27). Achsah realized water on her property would improve the welfare of her family.

> *Checkup:* Are you watching over your home? Are you aware of improvements that would enhance the welfare of your family?

Message #2: Improve. The wise woman enhances her property. Achsah noticed what her property needed to make it better.

> *Checkup:* Are you improving your residence (your house, room, or dorm room)? Do you have a plan of action (even for a good cleaning)? When are you going to start?

Message #3: Ask. Achsah knew what she wanted and needed to make her home improvements happen. She also knew the best person to ask—her father, Caleb, who owned the upper springs.

> *Checkup:* Do you ask God for wisdom, direction, and provision? Do you consult your husband? Do you check with others who might help you? Ask first and then act.

The Mark of a Remarkable Woman

Deborah, a prophetess...was judging Israel.
JUDGES 4:4

*T*he life and ministry of Deborah was truly extraordinary. Many lovely pearls of truth and wisdom comprise her remarkable beauty.

- *A remarkable woman*—Deborah was a prophetess, a wife, and a judge. She also went to war with the Israelite army, sang a song to the Lord, and was called "a mother in Israel"(Judges 5:7). No other woman in the Bible is described this way.

- *A remarkable calling*—Deborah is referred to as "a prophetess." Only a handful of women in the Bible were called to this lofty position.

- *A remarkable wife*—Along with the unique roles God called Deborah to fulfill, she was also "the wife of Lapidoth"(Judges 4:4).

- *A remarkable leader*—Deborah served in her home

and as one of God's judges over His people. Her leadership extended beyond her place of judgment—"the palm tree of Deborah"—to the plain of the battlefield where she was shoulder to shoulder with Barak, the army commander (verses 5 and 9).

- *A remarkable faith*—Although others wavered, including Barak, Deborah's faith in God's sure victory never faltered, even when the odds were against Israel.

- *A remarkable poet*—Inspired by God and from a heart of gratitude, Deborah sang. She offered a tribute to God (see Judges 5).

"Remarkable!" Does this rich word mark your life? While the specifics will differ, your commitment to God and your heart attitude can match Deborah's. How? Be diligent. Be devoted. Be dedicated. Be available. Be prepared. The rest is up to God!

Strength of Mind, Body, and Heart

Then Deborah arose and went with Barak [to war].

JUDGES 4:9

"Who can find a virtuous woman?" (Proverbs 31:10 KJV). Well, in Deborah God found one. A virtuous woman possesses power of mind (moral principles and attitudes) and power of body (ability and effectiveness). Deborah, a prophetess and judge in Israel, had both. She administered God's laws and managed and counseled His people. Strong physically, she accompanied Barak to the battlefield. While some may struggle with the mental image of a woman with a sword in her hand, God has nothing but praise for this remarkable woman and warrior (Judges 4–5).

The Hebrew word for virtuous is used more than 200 times in the Bible to describe an army. It also aptly describes Deborah. This Old Testament term refers to "a force" and means "able, capable, mighty, strong, valiant, powerful, efficient, wealthy, and worthy." The word is also used in reference to a man or men of war and men prepared for war. Simply change the masculine to the feminine, and you'll begin to understand the power at the core of a virtuous woman, the power at the core of Deborah.[11] To lead God's people into battle against their oppressors, Deborah called upon her mental toughness and physical energy, which are primary traits of a successful army.

The day-in, day-out duties you encounter call for you to be a virtuous woman of significant power of mind and body. Mental toughness and physical energy will keep you from giving up, giving in, dropping out, or quitting short of God's goals for you as you serve Him.

Take a moment to ask God for strength—His strength. Tell Him your desire to become a woman who moves through the challenges and duties of life with valor, courage, bravery, stamina, endurance, and power—His power.

"A Mother in Israel"

Deborah arose...a mother in Israel.
JUDGES 5:7

It's possible Golda Meir, former prime minister of Israel, knew about Deborah, a judge and leader of Israel. Golda Meir (1898–1978) once said, "I have no ambition to be somebody," and yet Mrs. Meir became great in her lifetime as she dreamed of a Jewish state and then witnessed its birth.[12] In her day Prime Minister Golda Meir was something of a mother to Israel.

The title "a mother in Israel" was originally attributed to the prophetess Deborah by God. Because of her roles among God's people as leader, judge, warrior, motivator, deliverer, and protector, Deborah became a spiritual mother to those in Israel. Her remarkable faith gave strength and courage to God's people. Her dedication to God enabled her to arouse the Israelites from spiritual lethargy. Her commitment to God and His people energized her to serve. Under Deborah's judgeship Israel enjoyed 40 years of rest.

Surely you too desire the remarkable, wholehearted

devotion to God Deborah had. Note these factors that contribute to a fervent, wholehearted commitment to God and foster great faith.

- *A life spent in God's Word*—All Scripture is profitable for instruction in righteousness. God's Word equips you for good works (2 Timothy 3:16-17).

- *A life spent in prayer*—To do great things for God, ask great things of God. The Bible says, "You do not have because you do not ask" (James 4:2). So ask for greater strength and perseverance, greater faith and devotion.

- *A life spent in obedience*—As you dedicate your life to being "a doer of the word," God promises you will be blessed (James 1:22,25).

Jael

Jael's Shocking Act

Most blessed among women is Jael.
JUDGES 5:24

*J*ael's story can, at first glance, cause confusion. The Bible praises her for assassinating someone! Let's unravel a few facts before we consider God's description of this woman who showed her love for God in a most unusual way.

- Israel was at war against the king of Canaan.

- Jael and her husband, Heber the Kenite, were dwelling in a tent about 15 miles from the battle.

- As Israel routed the Canaanite army, God's people pursued Sisera, the captain of the enemy forces.

- A tired and famished Sisera arrived at Jael's tent.

- While Sisera slept, Jael took a tent peg and drove it into his temple with a hammer (see Judges 4:17-21).

Although Jael's actions are startling and anything but lovely, God has nothing negative to say about her. Indeed,

God considered Jael a heroine, a woman who was "the friend of Israel." In their God-inspired song of tribute, Deborah, the reigning judge of Israel, and Barak, the captain of Israel's army, offer praise for Jael, the woman who was God's instrument for victory over Israel's enemy. They praise the faith of Jael, a foreigner, who acted out her faith in her family's tent in the only way she, a Bedouin tent-woman, knew. Using the tools and skills of her daily life, Jael battled for God in a time of war.

God gave praise where praise was due. File this distinctive "friend of Israel" story in your heart and pray for opportunities to help God's people and His purposes. I'm certainly not advocating violence or mayhem, but God may have some unusual plans for you.

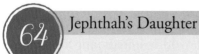
A Parent's Courageous Vow

His daughter [came] out to meet him.

JUDGES 11:34

*W*hat do parents who follow God dream for their children? That they will love God with all their hearts, souls, and might! If you have children, be diligent to...

- live in a way that reveals your love for God

- nurture them in the training and admonition of the Lord

- speak continuously of the Lord—when you're at home, in the car, before bed, when you wake up

Jephthah, the ninth judge of Israel, was called on to lead the Israelites into battle. He exhibited a heart of faith, "spoke all his words before the LORD," and was visited by "the Spirit of the LORD." Jephthah vowed that if God gave him victory, "whatever comes out of the doors of my house to meet me...shall surely be the LORD's, and I will offer it up as a burnt offering."

Unfortunately, when Jephthah returned home victorious, his daughter—his only child—was the first to come out to meet him. How did this godly father react? He tore his clothes and explained, "I have given my word to the LORD, and I cannot go back on it" (Judges 11:35).

How did Jephthah's daughter respond? Did she rebel? Run away from home? Scream? Throw a fit? Try to convince her father to compromise his vow to God? No, she chose none of these responses. By the grace of God, she honored her father and God's fifth commandment— "Honor your father and your mother" (Exodus 20:12). She affirmed her father's vow, saying, "If you have given your word to the Lord, do to me according to what has gone out of your mouth" (Judges 11:36).

When people—adults and children—live for God, there are always costs involved, along with the many benefits. As a parent, pray for wisdom and pray that your children's devotion to God will always grow despite any difficulties and hardships.

And a special word of caution: Be careful what you vow!

Hope That Shines in the Darkness

The Flower of Humility

His wife was barren and had no children.

JUDGES 13:2

*D*o you love flowers? Can the sight of a beautifully arranged floral bouquet take your breath away and stir your soul? As we stroll through the life of another woman of God, you'll notice a few of the blooms God, the Master Gardener, selected to make her life a lovely tribute to Him.

The first flower for this lovely woman's bouquet is the most fragrant—the flower of humility. Just as the fragrance for perfumes comes from crushed flowers, so the beauty and godliness of the wife of Manoah came from her humbling life circumstances. "Now there was a certain man...whose name was Manoah; and his wife was barren and had no children." These words can sear their way into a woman's heart, causing her head to hang and her soul to sigh. And this was especially true in the days of Manoah, when many people looked with reproach at those without children. Some even thought childlessness was punishment from God.

So what does a woman without children do? Identified only as "Manoah's wife," this woman probably spent time praying. We know her husband did. When Manoah's wife told him an angel appeared to her, Manoah prayed that the angel would return (Judges 13:8). Like other childless women of the Bible (Sarah, Rebekah, Hannah, and Elizabeth), this woman's inner pain presumably pressed her more closely to God.

What is your life situation? Is there something you deeply desire that has so far been denied? Is there something you yearn for? A life of faithful prayer has the lovely fragrance that comes from godly humility, from kneeling before Almighty God. Bow your head. Submit your soul. Allow God to do His exquisite work in your life.

The Flower of Faith

*And the Angel of the LORD appeared to
the woman.*

JUDGES 13:3

*T*he vase God selected for the flowers He graced the life
of Manoah's wife with is fit for an abundant bouquet.
Initially, it contained only a single stem—the bending-
but-fragrant flower of humility. But the Master was not
finished arranging the lovely existence of Manoah's wife.
A second rare blossom was added—the flower of faith.
Note its beauty—

"The Angel of the LORD appeared to the woman."
Whenever "the Angel of the LORD" appeared the occa-
sion was significant—and Manoah's wife paid attention!

The angel announced, "You shall conceive and bear a
son." Certainly this barren woman's heart leaped!

Next the angel gave Manoah's wife specific, personal
instructions: "Please be careful not to drink wine or similar drink, and not to eat anything unclean" (Judges 13:4).
These restrictions made up a Nazirite vow and set a person
apart for God's purposes.

The angel offered further instructions regarding the baby-to-be: "No razor shall come upon [your son's] head, for the child shall be a Nazirite to God from the womb" (verse 5).

Such an overwhelming moment! How did Manoah's wife cope? By faith. She asked no questions, requested no signs, and showed no hint of doubt. She responded with the rare and precious silence of belief. What a gracious flower of faith!

To add the delightful flower of faith into your life and character, love God with all your heart and study His Word. Trust in God's promises. Develop a faith marked by an accepting silence (no questions asked), a gentle spirit (no details needed), and a sweet submissiveness (no struggling against the unknown) to God and His will.

The Flower of Motherhood

So the woman bore a son.

JUDGES 13:24

*W*e often honor mothers with roses on Mother's Day. Here let's honor Manoah's wife with a single beautiful stem—the flower of motherhood. This blossom has been long in coming, and we rejoice with this formerly barren woman.

Known throughout the Bible as "Manoah's wife," at last another phrase can be used to describe this lovely lady: She's "Samson's mother." This gentle woman lived her life in the shadow of two men—her husband, Manoah, and her famous son, Samson, a judge of God's people and the strongest man who ever lived. Being a wife and mother appears to have been enough for her happiness and fulfillment.

Aren't you glad the Bible paints such a positive picture of parenting? From it we learn these divine truths about being a mom:

- Children are a heritage from the Lord (Psalm 127:3).

- The fruit of the womb is a reward from God (Psalm 127:3).

- [God] settles the barren woman in her home as a happy mother of children (Psalm 113:9 NIV).

The Bible also gives parents sound advice for raising children. Here are a few bits of wisdom:

- Train up a child in the way he should go (Proverbs 22:6).

- Bring [your children] up in the training and instruction of the Lord (Ephesians 6:4 NIV).

- Love your children (Titus 2:4).

If you're a mom, your calling is a high and noble one, a momentous stewardship as God entrusts precious children—His special creations—to you. Pray daily for your children. Teach them God's Word diligently, model Jesus, and worship together regularly.

A Future and a Hope

*[Elimelech and] his wife and two sons,
went to live for a while in the country of
Moab.*

RUTH 1:1 NIV

The famous opening words of Charles Dickens' *A Tale of Two Cities* declare, "It was the best of times, it was the worst of times." These words also describe ten years in the life of the woman Naomi.

The best of times. Because of a great famine Naomi and her family—her husband, Elimelech, and their two sons, Mahlon and Chilion—left their hometown of Bethlehem and settled in Moab where there was food. Yes, times there were good. They feasted and prospered. And, oh, how Naomi must have rejoiced when her two sons married. Each one met his mate in Moab. Those days were truly sweet!

The worst of times. But then the death knell sounded. First Naomi's beloved husband died, and then she lost her two precious sons—a triple blow to the heart of this wife and mom. How could something that had been so good turn so sour? Naomi seemed alone in the world...except for her sons' wives.

Have you felt like Naomi must have? Have you moved into what was supposed to be an ideal future, experienced temporary bliss and blessing...and then faced great loss and pain? If your answer is yes, God has two strong promises for you—

> "For I know the thoughts that I think toward you," says the LORD, "thoughts of peace and not of evil, to give you a future and a hope" (Jeremiah 29:11).

> And we know that all things work together for good to those who love God, to those who are the called according to His purpose (Romans 8:28).

As you cling to the One who made these promises, you will walk the path of "a future and a hope."

Learning to Trust

She went out from the place where she was.

RUTH 1:7

When you hit a hard place in life, it is not the time to collapse, cave in, fall apart, or break down. It is time to trust God!

The day Naomi and her family left their home in Bethlehem for Moab, Naomi "went out full." But tragedy struck. Her husband and then her two sons died. Naomi was devastated. When she heard the famine was over, she decided to return to her homeland. But it was a long journey.

- Naomi's daughters-in-law, Orpah and Ruth, started the journey with her.

- Naomi urged these young women to return to their respective parents' homes.

- Naomi kissed the two women goodbye.

- Orpah returned to her home.

- Ruth chose to stay with Naomi.

Certainly sorrow was not how Naomi envisioned her life, but she was learning to trust God more to work in her life through people, events, and circumstances.

- *The people*—Where once Naomi depended on her husband and sons, she would now depend on a young, widowed daughter-in-law.

- *The events*—Naomi certainly didn't choose to have her husband and sons die. But now she needed to trust God to work through their deaths.

- *The circumstances*—Never had Naomi imagined she would be returning home without her husband or sons. She would have to trust God.

God's Providence and Provision

She happened to come to...the field belonging to Boaz.

RUTH 2:3

*B*ethlehem was the place.
Food was the pressing need.
A field of grain was the setting.
Ruth was the woman.

There is no such thing in the life of God's children as happenstance or coincidence. There is only the great sovereignty of God Almighty who watches over His children and guides their steps, sometimes obviously and other times not.

In her new homeland Ruth, the daughter-in-law of the widow Naomi, ventured out to glean in the grain fields. She went without a guide, without a companion...alone except for God, who directed her steps to one particular field, owned by one particular relative, who would later become her husband! As you look at Ruth's life, consider this quote—

> God wisely orders small events; and those that seem altogether...[conditional] serve his own glory and the good of his people. Many a great affair is brought about by a little turn, which seemed...[lucky or accidental] to us, but was directed by Providence with design. [13]

Are you looking for God's hand in all the events, the coincidences, the chance happenings, the luck, and the flukes of your life? If you believe in a sovereign God, if you believe in His loving providence, you know that everything that touches your life is Him at work. So...

- look for the hand of God.
- believe God works in your life in all you encounter and experience.
- trust God to work all things, even "happenstance," together for your good (Romans 8:28).

71 Ruth

Sheltered by God's Wings

Under whose wings you have come for refuge.
RUTH 2:12

*T*he book of Ruth includes a pair of heartfelt "hymns."
  Ruth's hymn. Although raised in the pagan nation of Moab, Ruth placed her trust in the God of Israel. In her faith-filled declaration to Naomi, Ruth's words of devotion read like a song:

> Wherever you go, I will go;
> And wherever you lodge, I will lodge;
> Your people shall be my people,
> And your God, my God.
> Where you die, I will die,
> And there will I be buried.

Boaz's hymn. Boaz was a devout follower of God, a landowner, and a distant relative of Naomi. Upon meeting Ruth, he blessed her and encouraged her with a delightful melody of words:

The LORD repay your work,
and a full reward be given you
by the LORD God of Israel,
under whose wings you have
come for refuge.

Perhaps Boaz saw the struggling Ruth—a woman who had wandered into his barley field and labored diligently to gather food for herself and her widowed mother-in-law—as a fragile baby chick. In Psalm 36:7 God is portrayed as a mother bird who shelters her young chicks with her wings. What a tender metaphor Boaz used to bless Ruth for her remarkable hope and trust in God.

Are you trusting in God...and God alone in your daily life and difficulties? You can depend totally on the One who provides for His own. Your heavenly Father is responsible for protecting you. Your responsibility is to trust Him.

A Glimmer of Understanding

The LORD...has not forsaken His kindness.
RUTH 2:20

What would you do if...

- you were a widow,
- your sons died,
- your daughter-in-law was your only companion,
- you needed food?

This was Naomi's predicament. Too old to labor herself, Naomi depended on Ruth for the basics of life.

The law of Moses stipulated that grain dropped by reapers as they brought in the crops could be gleaned by the poor. This law was tailor-made for women in Naomi and Ruth's position. So Ruth went out daily to glean barley. One day she "happened"—by God's sovereign design!—into the field of a distant relative of Naomi's named Boaz. Boaz noticed Ruth and inquired about her. Then he introduced himself and blessed Ruth for finding refuge under the wings of the Lord. Boaz gave Ruth extended privileges when reaping in his fields. He also gave her extra food, extra grain, and protection.

When Ruth told Naomi of the goodness of Boaz, hope and joy pushed their way through the bitter, hard crust that encased Naomi's once-happy heart. "Blessed be he of the LORD, who has not forsaken His kindness to the living and the dead!" In Naomi's cold heart appeared a glimmer of understanding God's steadfast lovingkindness and His mercy.

God's gracious dealings offer at least two messages:

- Look for the kindness of the Lord extended to you through the good deeds of others.

- Extend the kindness of the Lord to others through your good deeds.

The Delight of Generations

Naomi took the child and...became a nurse to him.
RUTH 4:16

During her life Naomi traveled from a mountaintop existence of bliss into a deep, dark valley of sorrow—from the joy of marrying and living near family and friends to the abyss of moving to Moab, losing her husband, losing her two sons, and moving back to Bethlehem with one daughter-in-law. But God did not leave Naomi in her valley of despair. He did not leave her hopeless and empty. God blessed her with a grandchild, and she knew happiness again as she welcomed the warmth of a delightful grandbaby!

Tiny Obed was Naomi's first grandchild. Decades had passed since she'd held a little one in her arms. What did this babe signify to her?

- a continuation of the heritage of her husband
- a "son" to love after losing her own sons

- a child to care for and an opportunity to serve as nursemaid
- an offspring who would help care for her in her old age
- a "restorer of life" and a hope for the future

Being a grandmother is a great privilege! It also provides new opportunities, plenty of challenges, and myriad responsibilities. Here's a delightful acrostic to help you live out the "grand" in "grandmother."

Give a godly example

Remember important occasions

Always love your grandchildren's parents—no matter what

Never show favoritism

Develop a personal relationship with each grandchild

And if you're not a grandmother yet, pray for your own grandmother!

Precious Treasure

Now this is the genealogy of...Boaz.
RUTH 4:18,21

*P*roverbs 12:4 proclaims, "A virtuous woman is a crown to her husband" (KJV). And the widow Ruth was such a woman. After her first husband's death she married Boaz, a man of godly character. The union of this noble couple created a lineage that extended through time and for eternity. Take a moment to admire these gems in Ruth and Boaz's descendants.

"*Boaz begot Obed*"—As one Bible scholar noted, "Through the birth of Obed, God wove the thread of Ruth's life most intricately into the web of the history of His people. She became the chosen line through which later the Savior of the world appeared."[14]

"*Obed begot Jesse*"—Just as Isaiah had prophesied, "There shall come forth a Rod from the stem of Jesse, and a Branch shall grow out of his roots" (Isaiah 11:1). That Rod and that Branch was the Lord Jesus Christ.

"Jesse begot David"—The hope of a messianic king and kingdom was fulfilled in Christ through the lineage of David, his father Jesse, and his grandfather Obed, who was born to Boaz and Ruth.

Jesus Christ—The family tree or "the book of the genealogy of Jesus Christ, the Son of David" includes Boaz, Obed, Jesse, and David (Matthew 1:1,5-6).

If you have children or grandchildren, you are blessed! They are precious treasure and stars in your crown. Pray for them fervently. Encourage them in the Lord mightily. Ensure they know about Jesus abundantly. Support their spiritual growth heartily.

75 Hannah

Surrendering Pain to the Healer

He had two wives: the name of one was Hannah.

1 SAMUEL 1:2

Girls often dream of someday getting married. They may even spend years imagining and planning the perfect wedding day, honeymoon, and married life. In fact, most bridal magazines and books are purchased by young women who aren't even engaged or dating. These girls are simply fantasizing about their futures.

If, as a young girl, Hannah dreamed of the perfect marriage, her dreams were eventually met by harsh reality. She did marry, and her husband's name was Elkanah, a Levite from one of the most honorable families of priests. Hannah's husband may have been a terrific man, but there were some not-so-wonderful facts about Hannah's marriage to him. These dark threads of pain were woven throughout Hannah's life.

Hannah shared her husband. Hannah's husband had two

164

wives at the same time. (Yes, it was legal then.) Hannah's name is listed first, probably indicating she was Elkanah's first wife.

Hannah had no children. The Bible simply states, "The LORD had closed her womb." Hannah did not receive the blessing of children. Instead of ringing with laughter and the noises of active children, Hannah's house may have echoed with muffled sobs.

Hannah was harassed by the other wife. Insult was added to injury for the lovely Hannah. Peninnah, Elkanah's second wife and Hannah's rival, "provoked her severely, to make her miserable."

Gather together the dark threads of pain in your life and place them into the wise and wonderful hands of God. He will use them to make your life a beautiful masterpiece and testimony to His glory.

Shimmering Threads of Grace

I am a woman of sorrowful spirit.

1 Samuel 1:15

*I*n her pain—the pain of childlessness and the pain from cruel, relentless goading—Hannah turned to God. At the house of the Lord, weeping in anguish and bitterness of soul, Hannah prayed, crying out in her heart to the Lord rather than lashing out with her mouth. Never had she felt such agony. Never had she prayed so passionately. Never had she made such a serious vow to God.

As Hannah poured out her heart, the priest Eli saw her silently mouthing her cries to God. He concluded Hannah was drunk and reprimanded her, "How long will you be drunk? Put your wine away from you!"

And what was Hannah's response? Did she say "But you don't understand!" or "Wait a minute—that's not true"? Even though misunderstood and falsely accused, she responded gently. The soft hues of graciousness were woven into her life and were shimmering despite her difficult circumstances.

Hannah didn't argue or get defensive. She quietly explained, "I am a woman of sorrowful spirit." She knew and lived the truth of Proverbs 31:26—"She opens her mouth with wisdom, and on her tongue is the law of kindness." She followed God's wisdom for communication...

- Speak with wisdom and kindness (Proverbs 31:26).
- Think before you speak (15:28).
- Learn to speak softly (15:1).
- Add sweetness to your speech (16:21).
- Be instructive when you speak (16:23).
- Err on the side of less (10:19).

And how did Eli respond to Hannah's gracious speech? He gave her his priestly blessing.

Threads of Faith

Her face was no longer sad.

<small>1 Samuel 1:18</small>

At last Hannah's ordeal was over. Hope was glimmering on the horizon. Her trials had been many...and intense. Sharing her husband with another wife. Dealing with the heartbreak of being barren. Enduring harassment by the other wife. Being misunderstood by the temple priest.

But when Hannah explained to Eli about her prayer, she suddenly found her misery pushed aside by joy. What prompted this radical change? First Samuel 1:17 says Eli responded to her gentle explanation by giving Hannah a blessing with a promise: "Go in peace, and the God of Israel grant your petition which you have asked of Him."

A new color was woven into Hannah's life story. Perhaps the color blue to highlight her faith that spanned the sky and connected her to her heavenly Father. She placed her trust in God and the God-inspired blessing from Eli.

Nothing had really changed in her circumstances. She was still in a two-wife household, she still was not pregnant, and no doubt Peninnah would still harass her. But by faith Hannah believed in God and found joy in the promise of her petition being granted. After Eli pronounced his blessing, this woman who fasted, wept, and prayed in anguish and bitterness "went her way and ate, and her face was no longer sad." She didn't have a son—she wasn't even pregnant yet!—but she believed she would have a son someday.

Are God's threads of faith woven throughout your daily existence? Is your faith revealed in the everyday events of life? Faith is believing what God says He will do. Trust Him even when your situation doesn't seem to be improving. God is at work!

Hannah

The Brilliance of Joy

Hannah conceived and bore a son.

1 SAMUEL 1:20

*J*oy is brightest in the person whose life has been darkest. And dark, sad colors appeared throughout the life tapestry of God's servant Hannah. Yet suddenly there was a splash of brilliance! A new color—riotous threads of hope and joy—appeared. And it was quite a sizable patch!

Hannah knew dark times. She had marital problems because her husband, Elkanah, divided his love between her and another wife. She had personal problems as, year after year, she bore no children. She had people problems as Peninnah, the other wife who had given Elkanah several sons and daughters, relentlessly mocked and reviled her. And she had a problem in public when the temple priest scolded her for allegedly being intoxicated while praying from her heart.

But joy finally burst on the scene! Hannah received the priest's blessing and later conceived and gave birth to a baby boy. Never would she forget who had given her this precious baby. God, the Creator of life, heard her prayers and answered with the gift of a son. Hannah named him Samuel, meaning "name of God" and "asked of God," saying, "Because I have asked for him from the LORD."

Like Hannah, you can humble yourself before God and others, and pour out your soul to God, who sees in secret. Regardless of your circumstances, you can thank the Lord for His goodness and mercy. The psalmist calls us to "bless the LORD...and forget not all His benefits" (Psalm 103:2). So rejoice in the Lord always (Philippians 4:4). Rejoice in the forgiveness, redemption, and relationship with God that Christ made possible on the cross and through His death and resurrection. May these truths cause the brilliant threads of joy to brighten your darkness.

The Color of Giving

I...have lent him to the LORD.

1 SAMUEL 1:28

How the once barren Hannah cherished her little boy, never forgetting he'd been given to her by God. And she never forgot her promise to give her son back to God for a lifetime of service. She kept her vow as she lovingly raised little Samuel for the Lord. Finally the momentous day came when Samuel was to move to the Temple to serve God.

As Hannah and her husband approached the house of the Lord with their precious son and the required sacrifice, Hannah knew this day would require the most personal gift of all. She was giving God her best, most prized possession—her Samuel.

As you picture this family walking toward Shiloh, imagine the rich red threads added to the tapestry of Hannah's life. Red seems the most suitable color for sacrifice.

What can you give to God that reveals your love?

- Your children? God gave His only Son for you (John

3:16). Have you given your children to Him to use in any way and in any place?

- Obedience? "Has the Lord as great delight in burnt offerings and sacrifices, as in obeying the voice of the Lord? Behold, to obey is better than sacrifice" (1 Samuel 15:22). To what obedience is God calling you?

- Time? Every moment is valuable to God.

- Money? As he placed his silver on the altar, King David revealed his heart, "[I will not] offer...to the Lord my God...that which costs me nothing" (2 Samuel 24:24). Gifts of love cost.

Hold all things lightly and nothing tightly when it comes to God. "All" includes your best, most costly and cherished treasures.

A Vibrant Tapestry of Hope

Hannah...bore three sons and two daughters.

1 SAMUEL 2:21

*H*annah experienced great loss when she left Samuel at a very young age at the house of the Lord. Seldom would she see or interact with him after that time. Yet after fulfilling her vow to God, "the LORD visited Hannah, so she conceived and bore three sons and two daughters." Five more children filled Hannah's empty home after Samuel left. The seed of Hannah's sacrifice sprouted and bore much fruit. Hannah's faith grew, her family grew, her love grew, her joy grew, and her influence grew as she raised five additional children while Samuel was used mightily by God.

Can you see the vivid green threads of spiritual growth running through the weaving of Hannah's life? What can you take from her life to help yours become vibrant and strong?

- Hannah knew firsthand the heartache that

accompanies barrenness. Are you sympathetic and sensitive to those who have no children?

- Hannah took her problems to God. Do you tell Him your problems...or only your friends?

- Hannah faithfully communicated with the Lord. Have you learned the value of earnest prayer and petition (James 5:16)?

- Hannah discovered children are gifts from the Lord. How does seeing your children as God's gifts to you impact your parenting (Psalm 127:3)?

- Hannah understood the importance of training up a child for God. Are you diligently training your children—on loan to you from God—for service in His kingdom?

Wisdom and Strength for the Journey

The Strength of a Diamond

Abigail...was a woman of good understanding.

1 Samuel 25:3

*A*bigail. Mark this woman's name well. Her name means "cause of joy," and you'll experience great insights as you discover glistening diamonds made from dust—jewels of godly virtue—mined out of the adversity that filled Abigail's daily existence.

There was little cause for happiness in the soil of Abigail's life. Her marriage appears to have been loveless and childless. Her husband was a fool, "harsh and evil in his doings," "a scoundrel," and a drunk.

Yet the first dazzling, diamond-like quality we gather from the dust of Abigail's life is faithfulness. We see it in her loyalty, trustworthiness, steadfastness, and reliability. It is evidenced in her faithfulness to God's Word and to the people in her life. The Bible instructs God's women to build their homes and to watch over their households (Proverbs 14:13; 1:27), and Abigail did both.

When her husband foolishly refused to be kind to

the powerful warrior David, Abigail acted with wisdom quickly to appease the angry warrior and save the lives of her husband, her servants, and herself. The flashing diamond of Abigail's faithfulness glistened. Even in her problem-ridden situation, she was faithful to her husband, to her household, to her work in the home, and to God.

Does your life seem to be buried beneath generous layers of dust and dirt? Let your belief in God—regardless of your circumstances—shine brightly as you remain "faithful in all things" (1 Timothy 3:11). Never underestimate the brilliance and beauty of faithfulness in the eyes of God. After all, He is more concerned about you being faithful to His standards than He is about you being successful in the eyes of the world. And the people around you will notice your trust in God and be drawn to Him.

A Woman of Wisdom

Then Abigail made haste.
1 Samuel 25:18

"How could he do it? How could my husband say no to the mighty David?" Perhaps faithful Abigail thought this. She learned from her servants—who also couldn't believe what Nabal had done—that her household was at risk. David's band of men needed food so he sent his messengers to the wealthy Nabal. David's men treated the servants with respect as they asked for food. But Nabal, whose name means "foolish," turned him away! Since David and his warriors kept Nabal's shepherds and herds safe, Nabal should have gladly sent provisions. And now David was angry, and since he'd slain tens of thousands of people, keeping on his good side was the best thing to do (1 Samuel 21:11).

Abigail may have prayed, "What do I do, Lord?" And God granted her wisdom. With the help of her servants, she quickly sent David the food he had requested and more. Then she humbly approached David, bowing low. After offering him the food and drink, she begged for mercy and asked that David spare her foolish husband and their household.

When crises arise, be wise and take action—

- *Know the Lord.* "The knowledge of the Holy One is understanding" (Proverbs 9:10).

- *Fear the Lord.* "The fear of the LORD is the beginning of wisdom" (Proverbs 9:10).

- *Acknowledge the Lord.* "In all your ways acknowledge Him, and He shall direct your paths" (Proverbs 3:6).

- *Ask the Lord.* "If any of you lacks wisdom, let him ask of God...and it will be given to him" (James 1:5).

Be a wise woman. Ask God for guidance...*before* you take action!

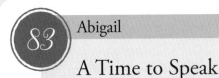

A Time to Speak

So she fell at his feet.

1 SAMUEL 25:24

Consider this paradoxical principle in Proverbs 25:15—"A gentle tongue breaks a bone." Abigail, a woman with beauty and brains, was caught in a face-off between two powerful men—her husband and the famed warrior David. When David needed food for his warriors, Nabal foolishly refused to provide it. And David foolishly decided to slay Nabal and destroy all that was his.

If ever there were a time to speak soft words that could break strong bones (and strong wills!), it was now. Approaching David, Abigail spoke gently, respectfully, and intelligently. She appealed to his future kingship, a purpose higher than revenge. However, with Nabal Abigail wisely waited to speak because he was "very drunk." He wouldn't understand what was happening or his narrow escape from death.

Abigail's discretion saved the day. She could have lost everything—including the lives of her innocent servants. She acted quickly and carefully. With both men Abigail exhibited good judgment in her timing, her choice of words, and her manner. Her gracious speech was effective, and the mighty will of the angry David was broken.

How can you improve in discretion?

- *Value discretion*—Understand its importance in human relations.

- *Desire discretion*—A mark of the wise is the desire for godly traits.

- *Learn discretion*—Study wise Abigail's discretion.

- *Use discretion*—Call on the Holy Spirit to help you exercise restraint and calm your emotions.

- *Pray for discretion*—Ask God to give you this valuable quality.

84 Bathsheba

Forgiven and Restored

She bore a son.

2 SAMUEL 12:24

*F*orgiveness! The sound of this comforting word brings joy to the heart of each and every repentant sinner. How we rejoice that our gracious and merciful God declared, "I will forgive their iniquity, and their sin I will remember no more."

Take a moment to consider Bathsheba, the wife of Uriah. The initial facts about her life hardly glow with godliness. In fact Bathsheba is best known for being an adulteress with King David. This sin resulted in her pregnancy, her husband's murder, and her newborn baby's death.

Yet like the sun after the rain, God's cleansing forgiveness shone brilliantly and warmly once Bathsheba's new husband acknowledged their sin. Hear David's words flowing from his penitent heart:

> I acknowledge my transgressions...Create in me a clean heart, O God...Restore to me the joy of Your salvation (Psalm 51:3,10,12).

After David's restoration to a right relationship with God, Bathsheba enjoyed the goodness of the Lord. Soon He blessed her with another baby, whom she named Solomon, meaning "beloved of the Lord." God chose Solomon to be king of Israel, and he is numbered among the ancestors of Jesus Christ (Matthew 1).

Everyone's life is spotted and stained with sin. Yet you too can enjoy the promise and reality of God's forgiveness. As one scholar wrote, "When we brood over sins God has said He will remember no more against us, we actually doubt His mercy and rob ourselves of spiritual power and progress."[15] No single sin should ruin an entire life. Instead, acknowledge your transgressions before God, receive His cleansing and forgiveness, and with joy over the salvation you have through Jesus Christ, enter a bright future.

The Right Time to Speak Up

Bathsheba went into the chamber to the king.
1 KINGS 1:15

A lovely line of Scripture prompts us to adorn our hearts with "the incorruptible ornament of a gentle and quiet spirit" (1 Peter 3:4). Does this mean we shouldn't speak up about issues? In the wife and mother Bathsheba we see there is "a time to keep silence, and a time to speak" (Ecclesiastes 3:7). She acted with discernment according to five principles that signal the time to speak up.

- *Find the right time.* David promised Bathsheba their son Solomon would reign as king after him. Yet David lay dying without naming a successor and unaware of an uprising in progress. It was time to speak up.

- *Choose the right issue.* If David's kingly line was to

continue through Solomon, he had to act immediately. The successor to the throne was the right issue to speak up about.

- *Act out of the right motive.* God designated Solomon as the man to build the house of the Lord instead of David (1 Chronicles 22:9-10). How could this happen if Solomon were not on the throne? This grand issue qualified as a right motive for speaking.

- *Be sensitive to the right prompting.* Nathan, God's prophet, approached Bathsheba, advised her to speak up, and told her what to say. The counsel of this godly man was the right prompting.

- *Speak in the right manner.* Bathsheba bowed respectfully, paying homage to her husband. She waited until he asked her to state her business. Humbleness and respect was the right way.

These principles are good for you to follow too. Try this approach the next time you must take care of business.

The Queen of Sheba

Searching for Wisdom

The queen of Sheba…came to test [Solomon].

1 KINGS 10:1

*I*n the sixth century BC news traveled slowly, ever so slowly—as slowly as people walk, camels amble, and donkeys shuffle. Slowly word of Solomon, Israel's wise king who served a powerful God, made its way to Sheba, some 1200 miles south of Jerusalem. Sitting in her palace, the queen of Sheba must have mulled over the various reports. Surely no person could be so wise and no god so remarkable! And yet…what if?

The queen decided to see for herself.

The trip to Jerusalem was long and expensive. Scholars estimate the progress of soldiers, gifts, animals, supplies, and attendants at 20 miles a day, so it would have taken 75 days. But no effort is too great and no price too high for true wisdom. With curiosity about Solomon, a willing spirit, and a deep hunger for wisdom, this queen set out for Israel.

What efforts are you willing to make to gain wisdom?

You could spend five minutes a day reading a chapter of Proverbs, the Bible's book of wisdom. You could attend classes, lectures, or seminars taught by wise and godly people. You could reserve time in your schedule to seek counsel or mentoring from someone you know to be wise.

We live in a drive-through, instant-gratification society. We want all things without effort—and we want them now! Yet in the example of this famous queen, we see a willingness to seek and sacrifice, to give whatever it takes to find answers to life's questions. Why not follow her example? Search for a precious pearl of wisdom today...and then add another to your strand tomorrow...and then another the next day. Wisdom is an ornament of grace to the soul.

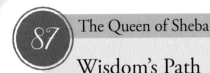

Wisdom's Path

King Solomon gave the queen of Sheba all she desired, whatever she asked.

1 KINGS 10:13

The queen of Sheba is truly worthy of admiration. Jesus even praised this exceptional "queen of the South." Why? Because when she learned of Solomon and his God, this woman decided to find wisdom. As one scholar noted, the queen of Sheba walked wisdom's pathway by taking these seven steps:

> Step 1: She heard—her ears were open (Proverbs 20:12).
>
> Step 2: She came with no regard for effort or expense.
>
> Step 3: She sought out and communed with the wisest man of her day.
>
> Step 4: She saw—her eyes were open (Proverbs 20:12).

Step 5: She said, "Blessed be the Lord your God!"

Step 6: She gave in gratitude for priceless wisdom.

Step 7: She returned home filled with the knowledge of God. [16]

As one who desires wisdom, follow these steps today... and for the rest of your life.

- Ask God. "If any of you lacks wisdom, let him ask of God...and it will be given to him" (James 1:5).

- Grow "in the grace and knowledge of our Lord and Savior Jesus Christ" (2 Peter 3:18).

- Desire "the pure milk of the word, that you may grow thereby" (1 Peter 2:2).

- Seek "those things which are above, where Christ is" (Colossians 3:1).

- Set "your mind on things above, not on things on the earth" (Colossians 3:2).

God will honor your efforts and bless you.

The Widow of Zarephath

A Measure of Faith

I know...the word of the LORD...is the truth.

1 KINGS 17:24

Have you sat on a beach and enjoyed the rhythm of the waves as they rolled up the sand? As one breaker swells and curls over, the next whitecap is forming with very little pause in between. Keep this image in mind as you remember the widow of Zarephath and how her story relates to your life. You see, your life has a rhythm too—the rhythm of trouble and trust. As the trials of life roll in, you have the opportunity to trust the Lord afresh.

The widow of Zarephath trusted God in a trial that threatened her little family's lives. When she had just enough flour for one last meal before death by starvation occurred, this dear woman used that tiny bit of flour—and her tiny bit of faith—to first make a bread-cake for God's prophet Elijah. Only then did she make one for herself and her son. In honor of her faith, God opened the windows of heaven and fed her, her son, and Elijah—for three years!

But then a new trial struck. This widow's little boy—her only child—died. As this wave washed over her fragile life, this desperate woman called on her faith to trust that God would help her again. She approached Elijah, and he raised the child from the dead. The widow's heart was revealed when she declared, "Now I know...the word of the LORD in your mouth is the truth."

Troubles never cease. They roll in as surely as the surf continues unceasingly, day in and day out. That's the nature of this world we live in. What are you facing today that you can give to God? Remember, God's mercy and compassion are new every morning. When troubles come, in faith reach out to Him. He will come through for you.

89

The Beauty of Usefulness

So [the king] made her queen.

ESTHER 2:17

What does it take to acquire the beauty of being useful to God? We get an idea from the life of Esther, an Old Testament heroine whose name means "a star."

Heritage—Esther, a Jew from the tribe of Benjamin, was taken to Babylon when her people were captives around 600 BC.

What have you learned from what your ancestors stood for, fought for, believed in, and endured?

Parentage—Esther's parents died while she was young, but a faithful and loving uncle brought her up as his daughter.

If you have "missing" parents, acknowledge those whom God provided in their place.

Tutelage—Esther was taught by her Uncle Mordecai and Hegai, a heathen eunuch in King Ahasuerus' palace.

Give thanks for the variety of teachers God has sent your way.

Advantage—Esther was gifted with physical beauty, Mordecai's wisdom, and Hegai's preferential treatment.

What circumstances and opportunities did God use to prepare you for working for His kingdom?

Homage—Esther's heritage, parentage, and tutelage garnered her honor when she was presented as queen.

Consider the honor you have and that you will receive in heaven because you are a daughter of the King!

Thank God for His active, transforming, loving presence.

Seven Steps to Wisdom

*What is your petition, Queen Esther? It
shall be granted you.*

ESTHER 7:2

Queen Esther learned that Haman received permission "to annihilate all the Jews" (Esther 3:13). How could she persuade the king to protect the Jews?

What a beautiful picture of strength, wisdom, and patience! Esther reveals how to effectively approach and persuade other people.

> Step 1: Stop. Before trying to rightly handle a wrong situation, Esther paused.

> Step 2: Wait. Time is a precious asset. Waiting gave Esther time to gather the facts.

> Step 3: Consult. Waiting allowed time for seeking further counsel.

> Step 4: Pray. Waiting gave Esther time to fast and pray for wisdom about how to approach the

king. She asked the Jews to do the same on her behalf.

Step 5: Decide. Time, counsel, and prayer moved Esther to choose a plan and move forward with the triumphant attitude "If I perish, I perish!"

Step 6: Act. Before she asked for what she wanted, Esther prepared a special dinner for King Ahasuerus and Haman to assess the king's frame of mind.

Step 7: Adjust. Discerning and sensitive to the situation, Esther wisely waited and prepared a second dinner before asking her husband to save her people.

When you face your next challenge, follow Esther's steps to wisdom.

Sweet, Gentle, Persuasive Speech

What is your petition, Queen Esther? It shall be granted you.

ESTHER 7:2

*W*hen we act with wisdom and patience, softness can indeed accomplish hard things. Because of a plot to kill every Jew, Queen Esther approached her husband to intercede for them. How did she go about it?

First notice what Esther didn't do. Nowhere in Esther's story will you find anger or agitation, violence or panic, rashness or reaction. Esther knew out-of-control emotions would not help her avert disaster.

Esther used sweet speech—a gentle tongue—to turn the heart of her husband against the instigator of the murderous plan. What were some of Esther's "sweet-speech patterns"?

- *Words of respect.* Esther addressed her husband respectfully, "If it pleases the king," "If I have found favor in [your] sight," and "I will do as the king has said" (Esther 5:4; 7:3; 5:8).

- *Words of welcome.* Esther sweetly extended an invitation to dinner, "Let the king...come today to the banquet that I have prepared for him" (5:4).

- *Words of caution.* Sensing the timing for her request wasn't right, Esther asked the king to return for another dinner the next day.

- *Words that were direct.* Esther boldly asked: "Let my life be given me at my petition, and my people at my request" (7:3).

- *Words few in number.* Esther's words were respectful, nonconfrontive, and direct. She chose her words carefully and said only what was necessary.

It is wise to pay attention to your speech patterns. May God grant you the beauty of sweet speech.

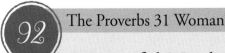

The Proverbs 31 Woman

A Powerful Mind and Body

Who can find a virtuous woman? For her price is far above rubies.

PROVERBS 31:10 KJV

God's use of the word "virtuous" in His description of a godly woman has a double meaning. Both aspects communicate positive strengths.

A powerful mind. "Virtuous" refers to a mind made strong by principles and attitudes. A quick glance at the woman in Proverbs 31 reveals how she uses it:

- She keeps herself pure (verse 10).

- Her husband trusts her, as do the people around her (11).

- She is a woman of industry (13,15,18).

- Ever thrifty, she provides for her loved ones (14).

- She faces life—and death—with courage (25).

- Compassion, kindness, and wisdom characterize her life (20,26).

- Holiness crowns her efforts as she honors the Lord in all she does (30).

A powerful body. "Virtuous" also describes this woman's ability to put into action what her powerful mind desires:

- She works willingly with her hands (13).
- She plants a vineyard (16).
- She operates a spindle and distaff (19).
- She works until late at night (15,18).
- She nurses the needy (20).
- She weaves the family's clothing (21-24).
- Never idle, she watches over and builds her home (27).

Ask God today to help you strengthen your mind and body.

Time-Management Tips for Your Day

She also rises while it is yet night, and provides food for her household, and a portion for her maidservants.

PROVERBS 31:15

*E*ffective time management is a challenge. There are seminars you can attend, time-management systems and notebooks you can buy, magazine articles that herald ultimate keys to success, and books proffered that promise busy women like you tools to handle the myriad responsibilities that fall to you.

But the best time-management help comes from God. He gave us His three pointers for perfect time management. You'll find them in Proverbs 31 as you watch a woman successfully walk through her busy day.

> *Step 1: An early start.* Getting up a little early each morning gave the Proverbs 31 woman a jump on the day and its to-do list. One of her first activities was tending the fire for

the day's meals and warmth. The early, quiet part of the day also allowed her to tend her heart's fire by spending time with God.

Step 2: Food for the family. Providing her family's daily bread was another important reason for rising early. Like your family, the Proverbs 31 woman's family depended on her for meals.

Step 3: A plan for the day. When the Bible says this woman gave a "portion" to her servants, it means she gave them their work assignments for the day. She diligently organized herself and her helpers so the housekeeping chores were accomplished efficiently.

God has given you the privilege of setting the pattern and tone for your household each new dawn. He will richly bless you as you seek Him early, see to your family's needs, and set in action a plan for the day.

94

The Proverbs 31 Woman

Dreaming, Planning, Taking Action

She considers a field and buys it; from her profits she plants a vineyard.

PROVERBS 31:16

Our all-wise Lord shows us more helpful pointers for being successful. The world of the Proverbs 31 woman extended beyond her home's doorstep—she was also a visionary and a businesswoman.

> Step 1: Consideration. Hearing that a certain field was for sale, this wise woman most likely prayed, asked questions of others, and sought advice from her husband about purchasing the field.

> Step 2: Acquisition. Blessed with peace of mind, practical answers to her questions, and her husband's approval, she took action. This prudent woman purchased her field with

money she had earned and saved through hard work and thriftiness.

Step 3: Renovation. With her hard-earned, well-managed, faithfully saved money, this capable woman improved her property by planting a vineyard with the best plantings her funds could buy.

Proverbs 31 calls us not only to labor, but to dream! This noble, accomplished woman dreamed—and then took action to realize them. She wanted a better life for her family, better and more food on their table, produce she could give and sell to other people, income she could invest to better her family, and the satisfaction of creatively bringing her dreams to fruition. She blessed others by using the abilities God had blessed her with.

Turn off the TV, the computer, and whatever keeps you from thinking creatively, from dreaming and wondering and planning. Take time before the Lord to jot down your dreams. Then consider (ask, seek, and knock), acquire (move forward), and renovate (improve your acquisition and grow your skills).

95

The Proverbs 31 Woman

Twelve Steps to Getting Things Done

She girds herself with strength, and strengthens her arms.

Proverbs 31:17

The Proverbs 31 homemaker worked hard to create a "home sweet home." What can you do to maintain a "can do," energetic spirit as you do the same?

- Embrace God's will for your life. The Proverbs 31 woman reflects His will for you.

- Stay in God's Word. There is power in the Word, so read it every day.

- Develop a vision. Create a "big picture" of what you want your home to be—a safe haven for family, a place to raise children who love God.

- Tap into the "why." Knowing why you do what you do helps keep you motivated to do what you must do wholeheartedly.

- Pray for an eager attitude. Ask God to help you accept with eagerness the tasks He has for you.

- Create a schedule. Plan and accomplish your work!

- Develop a routine. Routines help you fly through tasks and become more efficient.

- Read time-management books. Learn the best ways to do your job.

- Tackle the worst first. It makes the rest of your day easy.

- Play music. Upbeat music keeps you from sagging.

- See how quickly you can work. Make doing your chores a game. Beat the clock.

- Consider the blessings. Praise God for what your work means to you and those it impacts.

Pick one step, say a prayer, dig in, and enjoy getting things done!

96

The Proverbs 31 Woman

A Refreshing Fountain of Life-Giving Words

She opens her mouth with wisdom, and on her tongue is the law of kindness.

PROVERBS 31:26

Quenching thirst was a serious everyday challenge for the people in arid Israel. The basic struggle to survive was—and remains—the rule of the day there. Against this harsh backdrop Proverbs 10:11 says, "The mouth of the righteous is a fountain of life" (NASB). Godly speech is likened to water, which is essential for sustaining life. And godly speech meets emotional needs just as water meets physical needs. Words of wisdom and kindness will be to people like finding a fountain of sparkling water in the desert.

God uses very few words to describe the Proverbs 31 woman's speech. Two basic comments seem to nicely describe her:

Wise in speech—"She opens her mouth with wisdom."

Kind in heart—"On her tongue is the law of kindness."

Think again about that fountain of life in the desert. Then switch your focus to the hurting, stressed, struggling people you come into contact with or see in your daily world. While they may wear brave smiles, you know the truth behind every smile isn't always so pretty. Proverbs 14:10 and 13 (KJV) states, "The heart know[s] its own bitterness...Even in laughter the heart is sorrowful; and the end of that mirth is heaviness."

Ask God to use you to refresh and encourage the people you encounter today. Ask Him to bless you with life-giving words that are wise and kind and uplifting. With His love in your heart and the careful choice of words, you can help heal the downhearted and be as a refreshing fountain to their souls.

Growing in the Lord

*Charm is deceitful and beauty is passing,
but a woman who fears the LORD, she
shall be praised.*

PROVERBS 31:30

Underneath all we admire in the Proverbs 31 woman is her deep reverence for the Lord. Although our world values charm and beauty, God is concerned with our hearts. As you grow in your own love for Him, why not follow these time-honored practices?

Commit to Christ. In our New Testament age you can have a personal relationship with God through His Son, Jesus Christ. When Jesus rules your heart and life, everything you do is an act of worship done for Him (Colossians 3:23).

Schedule time with the Lord. As a believer in Christ you are privileged to behold His awesomeness and worship Him in the beauty of His holiness (Psalm 29:2). Set aside a regular, daily time to be in His presence for praise, meditation, and study. Time alone with the Lord is so essential and valuable!

Embrace God's plan and principles. Proverbs 31 lays out God's plan and principles for your life. So love Him and embrace His wisdom. Delight in every aspect of His plan, live His principles, and follow Him more fully every day.

Be sure. If you don't have a personal relationship with Jesus Christ or are unsure, take care of that now. Talk to Jesus. You can use the following prayer if you'd like. Set your foot on God's path. You will never regret it!

Jesus, I know I am a sinner. But I want to turn away from my sins and follow You. I believe You died for my sins and rose again victorious over sin and death. I accept You right now as my personal Savior. Come into my life and help me follow You from this day forward. Thank You!

Blessing Through God's Remarkable Provision

Mary, the Mother of Jesus

Blessed!

The book of the genealogy of Jesus Christ...Mary, of whom was born Jesus who is called Christ.

MATTHEW 1:1,16

We are introduced to Mary, the mother of Jesus, at the very beginning of the book of Matthew. In Jesus' genealogy she is referred to as Joseph's wife who will ultimately become known as the mother of our Lord and Savior.

Have you wondered why God chose Mary to be "blessed...among women," to carry within her womb God's Son, to love and cherish Him as her firstborn, to bring Him up in the knowledge of His heavenly Father? Here are a few things we know about Mary:

- *A chaste virgin*—The prophet Isaiah stated God's Son would be born of a virgin. Young Mary was unmarried and a pure, godly woman.

- *A humble maiden*—Hailing from the village of Nazareth, Mary was a small-town girl, not royalty or a sophisticated woman from high society.

- *A devoted follower*—Mary was a woman after God's own heart, a woman who would live according to His will.

- *A faithful Jew*—Of the tribe of Judah and the line of David, Mary worshiped the one true God and apparently did so in spirit and truth. Only such a woman would qualify for this important assignment from God.

What four phrases would you use to describe yourself? As you think about that, enjoy the relief that comes with knowing that no matter how humble, how simple, how poor, how ordinary, how intelligent, or how successful you are, God loves you! And like Mary, you can be blessed and used by Him to do great things. How? By loving Him...humbly, devotedly, faithfully, with all your heart, soul, strength, and mind.

Gifts of Encouragement and Vision

*They saw the young Child with Mary
His mother and fell down and worshiped
Him.*

MATTHEW 2:11

After Mary gave birth to Jesus, she welcomed "wise men from the East." Perhaps there was confusion when these exotic foreigners arrived and tried to explain their presence. These Magi saw "His star" in the East and came to worship Him. First they went to King Herod, the ruler of Judea, who was disturbed that someone besides him was deemed worthy of being called king. No one at court knew who this upstart was. But the Magi found out. At last the star that had directed them for hundreds of miles led them to Mary, Joseph, and Jesus. Surely Mary was encouraged by this visit from mysterious foreigners.

Vision—These men came to worship the Christ child, the King of the Jews. That they traveled several months from a faraway place probably gave Mary an even greater vision and clearer understanding of the future God had for her babe.

Provision—The wise men from the East paid homage to Jesus with valuable gifts. These gifts may have financed Joseph and Mary's flight-for-life to Egypt. Their hasty journey was to protect Jesus from the jealousy of King Herod, who ordered all Jewish baby boys in and around Bethlehem killed to eliminate potential rivals.

God knows His people's needs—including yours. Whether it's encouragement, a glimpse of what is to come, physical considerations, or something else, He has promised to "supply all your need according to His riches in glory by Christ Jesus" (Philippians 4:19). Look to Him. Lift up your needs to Him. The Lord is your shepherd; you shall not want! (See Psalm 23:1.)

100

Mary, the Mother of Jesus

Honored to Follow

> *[Joseph] took the young Child and His mother by night and departed for Egypt.*
>
> MATTHEW 2:14

*K*ing Herod was angry, jealous, and fearful when he heard someone was being called "King of the Jews"—even though it was a child. As a result he ordered the death of every Jewish boy under the age of two in the Bethlehem area to eliminate any potential rival.

We never know what marriage, motherhood, or even a given day will bring, do we? Mary—a woman who loved God, who was "highly favored" and "blessed...among women," who had found "honor with God"—also had lessons to learn about faith in God and following Him. God instructed Joseph, Jesus' earthly guardian, to take his family and flee to Egypt. What did this require from Mary?

> *Following her husband's lead.* Can you imagine being awakened in the middle of the night to hear your husband declare you're leaving— you're moving right now?

"But where are we going, Honey?"
"To Egypt. It's only a 10- to 15-day journey."
"But why?"
"I had a dream, and God told me to go."

Imagine what would happen under most roofs with this announcement! But we know Mary loved God and lived His plan so she followed her husband...and saved their young son's life.

> *Faith.* Faith in God enables you to follow God's plan. Adorn yourself with God's beautiful, gracious spirit and follow your husband or, if single, those God has in place to guide you.

> *Father, help me be a strong woman of faith, willing to follow my husband [or those in godly authority] as he leads me in Your good and acceptable and perfect will. Amen.*

101

The Mother of James and John

A Mother's Request

Then the mother of Zebedee's sons came to Him...kneeling down and asking something from Him.

MATTHEW 20:20

Today we meet the mother of James and John, the sons of Zebedee and two of Jesus' disciples. In this brief scene we see a caring mother bringing the desires of her heart before her Savior.

Person—There is no doubt that the mother of Zebedee's sons sensed Jesus' authority.

Posture—As this devoted worshiper approached her sovereign Lord, the only fitting posture was one of humility. This mother knelt before Jesus.

Petition—A faithful follower of Jesus, the mother of James and John asked Jesus to "grant that these two sons of mine may sit, one on Your right hand and the other on the left, in Your kingdom" (Matthew 20:21). In other words, "Give them special positions."

This faithful mom wanted her sons to love and serve Jesus forever. She may have misunderstood Jesus' teachings, but she does show spiritual concern for her sons. How are you doing on the three P's?

Person—Is Jesus your personal Lord and Savior? Are you obeying Him in every aspect of your life?

Posture—Do you nurture a posture of humility that honors Jesus as Lord? Are you a reverent and true worshiper? A woman of prayer and contrite in heart?

Petition—Do you bring every concern for your children to your heavenly Father? Do you ask, seek, and knock on behalf of your sons and daughters?

Pilate's Wife

The Flame of Understanding

*While he was sitting on the judgment seat,
his wife sent to him [...a note].*

MATTHEW 27:19

*J*esus generated quite a stir, the Jews in the High Council feared His large following so much so that they plotted His arrest. Judas, one of Jesus' disciples, betrayed Jesus and He was arrested. As Jesus stood before the governor of Judea, a messenger suddenly appeared with a note for Pilate. It was a warning from his wife: "Have nothing to do with that just Man, for I have suffered many things today in a dream because of Him" (Matthew 27:19). Astounding! She had...

- *a brief dream*—We don't know the particulars of the dream, but it was troubling enough to prompt a warning to her powerful husband.

- *a brief insight*—Her dream either revealed or helped her conclude that Jesus was a "just Man."

- *a brief note*—Acting quickly, Pilate's wife dashed off a succinct message to him.

Flickers of knowledge led this woman to intercede on Jesus' behalf. Did she have faith in Jesus? Did the light of understanding or insight last? Don't you hope so? And what about your understanding? Do you know...

- renewing your commitment to living for God daily fans the flame of faith?
- studying the Bible fuels an accurate understanding of God's Word?
- obeying in faithfulness causes your light to shine brightly among people?
- praying with passion allows you to see the blaze of God's glory?

Are you building a bonfire of faith?

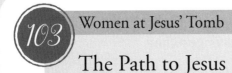
The Path to Jesus

Behold, Jesus met them...[and] they came and held Him by the feet and worshiped Him.

MATTHEW 28:9-10

*M*eet a small group of faithful women who witnessed Jesus' gruesome death. After three long, mournful days passed, they received the greatest blessing of all—they saw and spoke to the resurrected, glorified Jesus! Their story appears in all four Gospels, but only Matthew shares what Jesus said to these loyal ladies—words of reassurance ("Do not be afraid"), of instruction ("Go and tell My brethren"), and promise ("There they will see Me"). These women walked...

- *the path of faithfulness.* Most of Jesus' disciples deserted Him, but these women lingered at the cross to the end and then followed at a distance to see where He was buried. They later returned to the tomb to tend to His body.

- *the path of learning.* At the tomb on Sunday morning,

an angel instructed this little band of women to tell the disciples Jesus was alive.

- *the path of obedience.* Matthew tells us they departed quickly to carry out the angel's instructions. As they went in obedience to that divine order, Jesus met and spoke with them!

The women were awestruck, elated, and worshipful when they met their resurrected Savior—just like you would be in that situation! Can you picture it? The delightful shock, the smiles turning to grins, the laughter, the elation, the willingness to serve?

Does your relationship with Jesus inspire the same reactions? Do you need to reignite your faith through prayer, meditation, Bible study? Jesus was crucified for your sins, died, and was buried—then He rose from the grave, victorious over sin and death. And through Him you are too! Let your Savior know how thankful you are for His love and sacrifice.

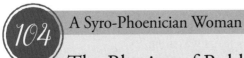
The Blessing of Boldness

She kept asking Him to cast the demon out of her daughter.

MARK 7:26

*A*rtists never depict Christ with His back turned," reports scholar Dr. Herbert Lockyer.[17] Yet in the book of Mark we meet an anguished mother Jesus refused to help. A pagan Syro-Phoenician woman was heartbroken as she watched her daughter suffer from a demon. She'd probably tried many ways to cure her daughter...to no avail. Was her hope waning? And then Jesus arrived in her Baal-worshiping region. She had heard of His kindness and powerful miracles. Did her heart leap as she thought, *Jesus can help!*

Humbly this dear woman sought out Jesus and fell at His feet. She asked Him politely and respectfully to cast the demon out of her daughter.

But Jesus refused.

Did she give up? No. She kept asking...and asking...and asking.

Jesus told her, "It is not good to take the children [of Israel's] bread and throw it to the little dogs [the Gentiles]."

With a flash of insight, this woman tried again. "Yes, Lord, yet even the little dogs under the table eat from the children's crumbs."

And then Jesus said, "For this saying go your way; the demon has gone out of your daughter." What relief and joy that mother felt! And when she arrived home, the demon had indeed left her daughter.

When you are suffering and in need, be bold:

- Place your faith completely in Jesus.

- Have enough faith to boldly ask...and ask again...and again...and again...for what you need.

- Know Jesus can and will help you.

- Trust in the power and efficiency of God and His Word.

Overcoming Hardship and Pain

His wife was of the daughters of Aaron, and her name was Elizabeth.

Luke 1:5

Meet Elizabeth, a woman from the priestly line of Aaron. She was married to a priest named Zacharias. In looking at their lives it's obvious they were both raised in families that feared the Lord and taught and practiced God's precepts.

Family devotion times are so wonderful and valuable. They bring your family together, encourage faith, teach God's principles, and equip members for handling life. The heritage of devotion to God helped Elizabeth walk bravely through a sometimes difficult and painful life. Starting with this reading and in the next three devotions, consider the benefits for gathering as a family in worship and study.

Reason #1 for a Devotional Time—"It will send you forth to your daily task with cheerful heart, stronger for the work and truer to

228

duty, and determined in whatever is done therein to glorify God."[18]

Elizabeth was childless. In fact, she passed the age of childbearing without having children. This means she endured decades of marriage under the dark cloud of barrenness in a culture that considered childlessness a calamity and possibly God's judgment for sin. How did Elizabeth keep going? Perhaps her faithfulness of spending time with God fortified her for the day-in, day-out painful reality of not having children. Regular time with the Lord enabled her to have a cheerful heart, strength for her work, and the determination to glorify God regardless of her circumstances.

Have you set a time for daily devotions? If not, begin today. Spend time each day being quiet before the Lord, studying His Word, and praying over your problems.

If you've been blessed with children, gather them every day to pray and hear God's Word. Encourage them to seek God in all they do.

Moment by Moment with God

They were both righteous before God, walking in all the commandments and ordinances of the Lord blameless.

LUKE 1:6

The elderly couple Elizabeth and Zacharias were blessed with a godly heritage, but they were also ordained to walk down a difficult road. They had no children— no little ones to love, no grandchildren to cherish, no one to carry on the family name. Despite this, Luke tells us Elizabeth and Zacharias were followers of God. They were...

- *Righteous*—Elizabeth and her husband followed God's law in strict legal observance.

- *Obedient*—Elizabeth walked alongside her husband in all the Lord's commandments (moral obedience) and ordinances (ceremonial obedience).

- *Blameless*—Elizabeth and Zacharias lived in a way

that pleased God. Outwardly obedient to the Law of Moses, they were also inwardly obedient to the Lord.

But still they suffered. Elizabeth shows us the way to love and follow God moment by moment when life is difficult. What contributed to her faithfulness? Probably daily time with the Lord.

> *Reason #2 for a Devotional Time*—"It will make you conscious throughout the day of the attending presence of the unseen Divine One, who will bring you through more than [a] conqueror."[19]

Throughout the day, moment-by-moment awareness of God's unfailing presence with you helps you bear every cross and face every crucible in victory through Christ. You can endure difficult times and remain righteous, obedient, and blameless if you believe in Jesus as Savior and look to Him for strength and wisdom daily, diligently, and devoutly.

Strength for Today

Elizabeth was barren, and they were both well advanced in years.

LUKE 1:7

The childlessness Elizabeth and her husband Zacharias knew may not sound too troublesome today, but in their time the Jewish rabbis believed and taught that seven kinds of people were to be excommunicated from God. Their list began with these searing words: "A Jew who has no wife, or a Jew who has a wife and who has no child." Besides being a great stigma in the Jewish culture, having no children was valid grounds for divorce!

But there was a heavier burden than the fear of divorce for childless women. Hebrew women hoped to bear the long-awaited Messiah. As a faithful, righteous, and obedient Jew, surely Elizabeth dreamed of being so privileged. Sadly the flame on Elizabeth's candle of hope died as her childbearing years flickered out.

How did Elizabeth handle this? Since her name means "God is my oath" or "a worshiper of God," surely she looked to Him for strength for each day.

Reason #3 for a Devotional Time —"It will bring you strength to meet the discouragements, the disappointments, the unexpected adversities, and sometimes the blighted hopes that may fall to your lot." [20]

As you face your day, look to the power of God to assist you with problems that arise. Time with Him—worshiping, thanking, asking, listening—provides the strength you need to face whatever comes your way. The love and wisdom you receive from the Lord will fuel your love and keep the flame of hope burning. Cling to God's promise, "Be strong and of good courage; do not be afraid, nor be dismayed, for the Lord your God is with you wherever [and through whatever!] you go" (Joshua 1:9).

Miracles and Blessings

*Now after those days his wife Elizabeth
conceived; and she hid herself five months.*

LUKE 1:24

God provided a miracle! No, many miracles!

First miracle—An angel said, "Your prayer is heard and your wife Elizabeth will bear you a son...he will be great in the sight of the Lord."

Second miracle—Zacharias questioned the angel's glad tidings and lost his ability to speak...until his son's birth.

Third miracle—Elizabeth conceived in her old age.

How did Elizabeth respond to the miracle of pregnancy? Did she boast and tell everyone? No. She stayed home. Why?

- *She was joyful*—A baby was on the way! And this baby would be the forerunner of the Messiah.

- *She was grateful*—She probably spent much time at home bowed in thanksgiving before God.

- *She was realistic*—The expected child was to play a mighty part in the history of God's people, and the responsibility of training him in godliness demanded serious and prayerful preparation.

Do you go to the Lord with your sorrows *and* your joys, your gratitude and your responsibilities, your hopes for today and your dreams for tomorrow?

> *Reason #4 for a Devotional Life*—"It will sweeten home life and enrich home relationships as nothing else can do."[21]

God fills you with His love and hope, peace and strength when you spend time with Him. This blesses you, those you live with, and those you meet.

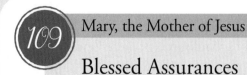

Blessed Assurances

Then Mary said to the angel, "How can this be?"

LUKE 1:34

The sun rose that morning just as it had risen every day. As she considered her list of chores, she had no hint that her life was about to be transformed from the mundane to the mysterious.

Seconds after it happened Mary's hopes for a quiet, peaceful life were gone. Gone also were the comfort and safety of predictable routine. What happened? The angel Gabriel appeared before young Mary and delivered an earth-shattering message. Nothing would ever be the same for Mary or the world. God chose her to be the mother of His Son. She would bring into the world its Savior, Lord, and King.

How did Mary handle this great turning point in her life? And what life lessons can we garner from her experiences?

We see in the Gospel of Luke that Mary humbly accepted the news that she would bear God's Son. Notice her initial response—"How can this be, since I am a virgin?" (NASB). This perfectly natural question received an answer that pointed to the supernatural: "The Holy Spirit will come upon you, and the power of the Highest will overshadow you; therefore, also, that Holy One who is to be born will be called the Son of God." The birth would be a miracle. And that was all the explanation Mary received.

Can you point to a day in your life that changed everything? Maybe a dark cloud hid the sun. Or the day was so bright you had to cover your eyes. Such turning points can shake us to the core. And they can send us to God, His Word, and His promises in praise for what He's brought, or to the acceptance that sometimes the full understanding of the "hows" and "whys" lies in the realm of God. [22]

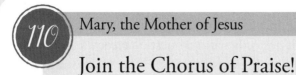

Join the Chorus of Praise!

Mary said: "My soul magnifies the Lord."
LUKE 1:46

The surest test of a heart is the caliber of its speech—the quality of the words that issue forth. Through Mary's words we see her pure heart. As she arrived at her cousin Elizabeth's home, this young woman opened her mouth and offered rich words of praise, a song now known as Mary's "Magnificat." Mary began, "My soul magnifies the Lord," and the inspired words that follow contain 15 quotations from the Old Testament (Luke 1:45-55). As one author observed, the number of Scriptures quoted in the "Magnificat" shows that "Mary knew God, through the books of Moses, the Psalms and the writings of the prophets. She had a deep reverence for the Lord God in her heart because she knew what He had done in the history of her people."[23]

Clearly Mary's heartstrings were tuned to the heart of God. Her heart was saturated with His Word. Knowing God and His remarkable provision, mercy, and faithfulness, Mary sang...

- a song of joy, of gladness, of celebration.

- a song of substance based on the Scriptures.

- a song reflecting the love and devotion of Hannah, a saint from the past (1 Samuel 2).

- a song for today since God is the same yesterday and today.

- a song for eternity because God's Word stands forever.

Because you know God and recognize His infinite power and love, you can join Mary in her chorus of praise. Read her beautiful and joyful words and add your voice to her sweet melody, "My soul magnifies the Lord!"

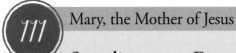
Standing on a Foundation of Blessing

Holy is His name.

LUKE 1:49

*D*o you long to be a woman of great faith? If so, fill your heart and mind with the Word of God. Mary, Jesus' mother, obviously had great faith because her words reveal a heart overflowing with Old Testament law, psalms of praise, wisdom from the prophets, and prayers of believers...

- *God's holiness*—"Holy is His name!" God is wholly pure in total contrast to sinful, self-centered humans. In Jesus, God revealed His holiness (Luke 1:49).

- *God's mercy*—"His mercy is on those who fear Him from generation to generation." In Jesus, God extended His mercy by providing for our salvation (verse 50).

- *God's power*—"He has shown strength with His arm; He has scattered the proud in the imagination of their hearts. He has put down the mighty from their thrones, and exalted the lowly" (verses 51-52). Stand in awe of God's power.

- *God's goodness*—"He has filled the hungry with good things, and the rich He has sent away empty." God is good, and Jesus' life and teachings reflect His desire to reach out to everyone (Luke 1:53; 6:35).

- *God's faithfulness*—"He has helped His servant Israel, in remembrance of His mercy, as He spoke to our fathers, to Abraham and to his seed forever." God is eternally faithful to His Word and to His chosen people. In Jesus, God sent the Redeemer He promised to Abraham and to us as Abraham's seed (Luke 1:54-55).

Rejoicing in God's Goodness

Elizabeth's full time came...and she brought forth a son.
LUKE 1:57

God, who is mighty, performs great things for those who love Him. The barren Elizabeth's "great things" included a miraculous pregnancy in her old age and the birth of her son, John the Baptist. "When her neighbors and relatives heard how the Lord had shown great mercy to her, they rejoiced with her" (Luke 1:58).

Imagine Elizabeth's complete and utter joy at God's goodness to her. She'd been so long without a child and then, miracle of miracles, God chose her to bear John, the forerunner for the Lord. Elizabeth's little baby would be great in the sight of the Lord, filled with the Holy Spirit, turn the hearts of many to the Lord, and herald the coming of the Messiah. The blazing light of God's goodness made decades of darkness fade into a distant memory.

Do you often think about the great things God has

done for you? Elizabeth hid herself for five months to contemplate God's goodness.

If you're a mother, consider that one of life's greatest blessings. Children are a source of great joy. When John was born, his mother's heart was filled with overflowing joy.

Make it a habit to rejoice with others over the great things God does in their lives. Elizabeth's neighbors rejoiced with her.

Rejoice in God's goodness. Be faithful to God and trust in His goodness even when you can't see obvious signs of His love. Remember Gods people "walk by faith, not by sight" (2 Corinthians 5:7). Choose to trust in God's redemptive goodness and unfailing love.

Being Blessed Doesn't Mean a Carefree Life

Yes, a sword will pierce through your own soul also.

LUKE 2:35

*N*one of us knows what the future holds, but God gave Mary a hint about what awaited her—"a sword would pierce her soul." Mary was highly favored by God and greatly blessed to be the mother of His Son, but this privilege also meant real trials.

When Mary and her husband Joseph took Jesus to the temple to dedicate Him to God surely their hopes and dreams soared as they considered His bright future. Affirming their thoughts, an old man named Simeon—a devout man of God who worshiped regularly and waited expectantly to see the coming of the Lord—took Jesus in his arms and prophesied concerning His ministry to the world. But as Simeon finished his blessing, he turned to Mary and said, "A sword will pierce through your own soul also." Mary must have wondered what that meant. What was going to happen that would cause her so much pain?

We will never fully know the depth of Mary's anguish, but Simeon's words paint a gruesome picture. The word for "sword" is the same one used in the Old Testament to describe the giant Goliath's large weapon (1 Samuel 17:51).

God's great blessings don't guarantee a carefree life. They often come at the cost of our personal comfort. But the more we listen and follow Him, the more He can transform us and those around us so His messages of love and salvation are known. Perhaps this cost is why the Bible encourages God's people to highly regard those we may be tempted to envy. We are to...

- rejoice with those who rejoice.
- esteem those who rule over us in the Lord.
- pray for those who rule and obey them.

We don't always know the price of God's favor, but we do know His love and favor are worth the cost.

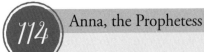

The Gift of Shared Light

Now there was one, Anna, a prophetess.
LUKE 2:36

*P*rophetesses were empowered to speak God's Word,
bringing light into darkness—

Miriam led the Israelite women in praise when God
defeated the Egyptian Pharaoh and his army (Exodus
15:20).

Deborah served as a judge in Israel and gave Barak
instructions from God that led to victory against Sisera
(Judges 4:4-7).

Huldah counseled King Josiah regarding the book of
the law (2 Kings 22:14).

Now we meet Anna. After the Prophet Simeon made his
somber pronouncement regarding Jesus' future and Mary's
suffering, Anna, a prophetess, "gave thanks to the Lord,
and spoke of Him to all those who looked for redemption in Jerusalem." Perhaps Anna's words momentarily

lifted the dark cloud that crossed Mary's happy heart with Simeon's dark warning.

Anna's life was touched by darkness. Her dear husband died young and for many, many years she daily lifted her eyes to the hills and looked for the coming of the Messiah. And behold, in time the Light of the world entered the temple! Mary arrived, carrying the long-awaited Christ child in her arms—the One who would dispel the world's darkness. No wonder Anna praised and thanked God!

How gracious of God to use Anna to remind Mary that her dear son—her Savior, her Lord, and her Master— would bring the brilliance of His light to her needy heart. Everyone needs light—the light of God's Word, the light of the gospel, the light of His promises, and the light of joyful trust in Him. Won't you share that light with someone today?

A Refreshing Balm of Encouraging Words

[She] did not depart from the temple, but served God with fastings and prayers night and day.
LUKE 2:37

*I*n just a few verses God gives us all we know about Anna, a prophetess and a godly woman who loved God into her sunset years.

Anna was a widow. Having lost her husband after only seven years of marriage, this woman knew sorrow. But she apparently allowed her suffering to soften her fiber and strengthen her faith. Anna spent her long life in faithful service to the Lord night and day.

Anna was a senior citizen. At age 84 Anna still looked for "the deliverance of Jerusalem," for the Messiah, for the Savior—for Jesus! How truly blessed she was when God rewarded her many years of faith by allowing her to see—in the flesh—the Hope of Israel!

The life of Anna offers us two important lessons. First, we see the fruit of long-term faith, of faith that "is the substance of things hoped for" (Hebrews 11:1). Is your faith ever-burning? Never dimming, never cooling, never faltering as you look to God for the hope of Jesus' Second Coming?

Also, we learn about encouraging one another. How Anna's joyous outpouring of faith must have sunk deeply into Mary's confused soul after Simeon prophesied that she would encounter sorrow. Anna's words of encouragement were a balm of refreshment to her bruised spirit.

Lift up and encourage someone who is cast down today. Speak timely words of ever-burning faith in God to those who are weary.

Faithfulness
in All Things

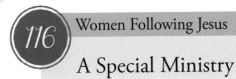
A Special Ministry

Certain women...provided for Him from their substance.

LUKE 8:2-3

When our Lord Jesus walked this earth "certain women" enjoyed a role "absolutely unique in the gospels," explains theologian Charles Ryrie.[24] They ministered to the Lord—a role that His male followers and disciples didn't have. We more fully appreciate the specialness of this role when we realize the Greek word used here for serving appears in the four Gospels only when the ministry or service is being rendered directly to Jesus. In those cases it is administered by either angels or women!

Who made up this honored band of faithful followers? Mary Magdalene, Joanna, Susanna, and "many others." These women chose to follow Jesus and support His ministry, giving of their substance and their service.

Substance. By funding Jesus' ministry and supporting Him and His disciples as they preached, these women met a very practical need.

Service. Graciously and unobtrusively, these dear women also saw to Jesus' personal comfort and well-being.

Today we serve the Lord by serving His people. As one scholar noted regarding our service to those who labor for the Lord, "It is not always the person in the foreground who is doing the greatest work. Many a man who occupies a public position could not sustain it for one week without the help of [others]. There is no gift that cannot be used in the service of Christ. Many of His greatest servants are in the background, unseen but essential to His cause."[25]

Think of three specific ways you can advance Christ's cause through your substance and service. Write them down and commit to doing them. Jesus said, "Inasmuch as you [helped] one of the least of these My brethren, you did it to Me" (Matthew 25:40).

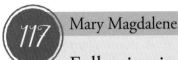

Mary Magdalene

Following in the Lord's Shadow

*Mary called Magdalene, out of whom
had come seven demons.*

LUKE 8:2

*H*ave you heard the saying "the worst first"? Well, in the book of Luke we find a roster of women who served Jesus and were healed and delivered by Him. "The worst" is the first to be named—Mary Magdalene, who was delivered from seven demons. Can you imagine the pain, the torment, the destruction Mary suffered?

Jesus, the God of compassion and power, delivered this desperate woman. The details of Mary's "seven demons" and that she was from the town Magdala on the Sea of Galilee are the specifics we are given. But from the moment of her release she appears to have followed Jesus. She who was delivered from much loved much.

Because of Christ the past has no hold on our present or our future. Consider these truths:

- "Therefore, if anyone is in Christ, he is a new creation; old things have passed away; behold, all things have become new" (2 Corinthians 5:17).

- "It is no longer I who live, but Christ lives in me" (Galatians 2:20).

- "I press on...forgetting those things which are behind and reaching forward to those things which are ahead" (Philippians 3:13-14).

- "Set your mind on things above, not on things on the earth. For you died, and your life is hidden with Christ in God" (Colossians 3:1-3).

Choose one of these passages and memorize it. Hide its freeing truth in your heart. Like Mary Magdalene, you can—in God's power—rise up from your past and press on as a faithful follower of Jesus.

Jairus' Wife

When Hope Is Gone, Walk by Faith

He permitted no one to go in except...the father and mother of the girl.

LUKE 8:51

The multitude of people surrounding Jesus had so many needs. Among them were Jairus, the ruler of the synagogue, whose 12-year-old daughter was dying, and a woman who had a continual issue of blood. Only God could meet such needs, so Jesus, God-in-the-flesh, healed the dear woman who now worshiped at His feet. Her 12-year-long hemorrhage ended. A messenger arrived and told Jairus his daughter had died. But Jesus assured Jairus that his daughter would be restored...if he would "only believe." But what about Jairus' wife, the little girl's mother?

When Jairus went to get Jesus, the anxious mother tended to their dying daughter, doing all she could—hoping...praying...waiting. The agonizing minutes dragged on and on. Where was Jesus? Her hope died when she witnessed her beloved daughter's final breath. Perhaps this devastated mother sent the messenger to her husband to let him know it was too late. Perhaps she also called in the mourners who began their vigil.

Despite the message, in strode the Healer, filled with strength and power and honor and glory and majesty. Jesus dismissed everyone but the girl's parents and His three closest disciples. He took the dead child's hand and spoke: "Little girl, arise." Her spirit returned, and she arose immediately!

You must believe God's Word regardless of life's events, regardless of hopeless circumstances, regardless of what appears to be, regardless of timing and events that go wrong. Don't look at what you can see, but look to the things that are not seen, "for we walk by faith, not by sight" (2 Corinthians 4:18; 5:7). While you hope and pray and wait, trust in the Word of God.

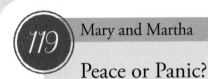

Peace or Panic?

Martha welcomed Him into her house.
And she had a sister called Mary.

LUKE 10:38-39

We face so much stress and pressure today. We never seem to have enough time—pressure. We want to do well as a wife and a parent—pressure. We are called to be good stewards of finances—pressure. We strive to be effective managers of our homes—pressure. How do we handle all the pressures of life and experience peace instead of panic?

In the sisters Mary and Martha, God gives us a classic study in opposites. Jesus went to their home for dinner. Martha welcomed Him in, but then she became distracted by all the preparations. Busy in the kitchen with lots of details on her mind and anxious that everything go well, Martha was a whirlwind of activity. Was she at peace? No.

How did her stress show? Martha was stirring the pot in the kitchen, but she was also stirring things up in the family room. There she accused Christ ("Don't you care?") and accused Mary ("She's left me to serve alone"), complaining about the burden of dinner. Martha was bossy, blaming, distracted. She was "yarping"—which, you'll notice, is "praying" spelled backward!

In contrast to this hurricane of hyperactivity, we find Mary...

- resting at the Lord's feet while Martha is restless
- worshiping while Martha worries
- remaining at peace while Martha's panic level rises
- sitting while Martha is stewing
- listening while Martha is lashing out

What was Jesus' response? He commended Mary for doing what is most important—spending time with Him.

Would an outside observer see Martha or Mary in you as you deal with schedules, commitments, and pressures? Do you need to make any changes?

Widow with Two Mites

Surrendering All

He saw also a certain poor widow putting in two mites.

LUKE 21:2

I surrender all...

> All to Thee I freely give...
> I surrender all![26]

These simple words from a well-known hymn touch a chord deep within our hearts. We are called by God and privileged to relinquish our all to Him, to fully accept His perfect will, and to live "the surrendered life." In Luke 21 we come face to face with a woman who truly did just that.

As Jesus sat in the temple area, He watched many people deposit money into the collection boxes. These gifts were for the day-in, day-out operation and upkeep of God's temple. The rich were openly putting in their large gifts. But what caught Christ's eye was a poor widow quietly putting in two small coins. In His omniscience Jesus knew how many and how much. Her gift was two mites, or two lepta, two of the smallest coins in existence, two of "the thin ones."

But Jesus knew something else as well. Perhaps clearing His throat before He spoke, He stated to those around Him, "Truly I say to you that this poor widow has put in more than all; for all these out of their abundance have put in offerings for God, but she out of her poverty has put in all the livelihood that she had" (verses 3 and 4).

Jesus' praise for this dear widow's sacrificial giving is forever preserved in God's Word. This woman and widow of poverty—this woman with few resources—gave all she had.

God's word instructs us to give regularly, freely, and sacrificially. How much you give of what you have and how you give those gifts are the true measures of your love for God. As Jesus said, "Where your treasure is, there your heart will be also" (Matthew 6:21). Where is your heart?

Faithfully Following Jesus

Then they returned from the tomb and told all these things to the eleven and to all the rest.

Luke 24:9

We talk about, we desire, and we pray for a life spent faithfully walking with Jesus. The circle of women who loved Jesus and faithfully followed Him to the end shows us what it means to truly follow Him.

- *They followed Him in life.* As Jesus ministered throughout Jerusalem, Judea, and Samaria, these women ministered to Him (Luke 8:2-3).

- *They followed Him after He died.* This faithful band of women waited at the foot of the cross, watched as His body was removed, and walked to the tomb.

- *They followed through in duty.* These dear women realized that Jesus' body was not properly prepared for burial. The next morning, as they followed through on this final duty to their departed Friend, they were blessed to be the first to witness His resurrection from the dead and to talk with the risen Lord (John 20:11-18)!

- *They followed His instructions.* When they spoke with Jesus, He said to tell His brethren all these things (John 20:17), and they rushed to do just that!

True discipleship requires that you follow Jesus in life, in death, in duty, and in obedience. Make the words of this old familiar hymn, "He Leadeth Me," the prayer of your heart.

> He leadeth me, He leadeth me.
> By His own hand He leadeth me.
> His faithful follower I would be,
> For by His hand He leadeth me.[27]

"He Who Believes in Me"

*Then Martha, as soon as she heard that
Jesus was coming, went and met Him.*

JOHN 11:20

An "odd couple" consists of two people who handle life in contrasting ways. Sisters Mary and Martha certainly qualify! When Jesus visited, Martha bustled with unbridled energy while Mary was content to worship at His feet. Today we see this "odd couple" in another situation. Their brother, Lazarus, was seriously ill. The sisters sent for Jesus, but He didn't come and their brother died. When the sisters heard Jesus was approaching their village, how did Martha respond? True to form, she leaped up, rushed out the door, and ran down the road to meet Him.

Martha's statement of faith. Martha may have been abrupt and hurried, but her heart was right. She believed in Jesus and trusted in His power to heal. "Lord," she ventured when she met Him, "if You had been here, my brother would not have died."

Martha's lesson in faith. Martha was right to go to Jesus, but she missed a central truth about Him. When she volunteered, "I know that whatever You ask of God, God will give You," Jesus corrected her by stating, "I *am* the resurrection and the life. He who believes in Me, though he may die, he shall live." He was saying, "Martha, I don't have to ask of God. *I am God!* And life is in Me. He who believes in Me shall live."

Martha recognized Jesus' power, but her understanding of His deity was incomplete until He corrected her. Do you believe Jesus is God—God-in-the-flesh—and that belief in Him, though you die physically, gives you eternal life? That is the message Martha heard from the lips of Jesus, and it is His message to us too. Jesus asked Martha, "Do you believe this?" Do *you?*

Mary and Martha

Offerings of Worship and Adoration

There they made Him a supper; and Martha served [and] Mary...anointed the feet of Jesus, and wiped His feet with her hair.

JOHN 12:2-3

*B*efore we bid Mary and Martha Godspeed, let's peek through a window. The whole family is at home—Mary, Martha, and Lazarus, whom Jesus raised from the dead. We see a truly joyous celebration as these grateful folks prepare another meal for their beloved Jesus. The scene is both priceless and instructive.

Service. As usual, Martha served. Are we surprised? Service is Martha's way of expressing love. She was a practical woman. She delighted in actively meeting the needs of Jesus and the other people she loved.

And you? Are you faithful to serve where God places you, remembering that whatever you do, you are to do it heartily "as to the Lord and not to man" (Colossians 3:23)? Do you regard the practical tasks at home—meals to prepare, floors to sweep, clothes to wash—as expressions of your love for God? While these daily duties may seem mundane, God knows the sacrifice involved and is pleased when we serve as unto Him.

Worship. As usual, Mary worshiped. Again, are we surprised? This evening she poured her expensive oil over Jesus' feet in an act of extravagant love and then wiped His feet with her hair.

Are you a passionate worshiper of God? Your acts of adoration may be scoffed at, as were Mary's, and people may consider your worship unwise, your sacrifice of finances and time wasteful, your activities for Him foolish. But God welcomes every gift and offering of worship you bring!

Living with an Open Heart

*Lydia heard us... The Lord opened her
heart to heed the things spoken by Paul.*

ACTS 16:14

*L*ydia was a very influential and take-charge woman. Into her heart were sown the seeds from which the church at Philippi grew. Consider some of the threads that make up the tapestry of Lydia's life.

- *She was a woman.* This obvious fact is important. You see, ten *men* were required to organize a synagogue, and apparently this quorum was missing in Philippi. Not having a synagogue in which to gather, the women met outside the town to pray.

- *She was a worshiper.* Lydia believed in the God of Israel, but she had not yet become a follower of Jesus Christ.

- *She was attentive.* One day down by the river the apostle Paul showed up at the women's prayer meeting, sat down, and began talking about Jesus. Lydia listened.

- *She was baptized.* As the truth about Jesus Christ penetrated Lydia's open heart, she accepted God's gracious gift of salvation. The first thing she did as a Christian was to get baptized.

- *She was influential.* Lydia was not baptized alone. Evidently she was instrumental in her entire household—relatives and servants alike—becoming believers.

- *She was hospitable.* Not only did Lydia open her heart, but she also opened her home. Paul's message had helped her, and now she wanted to help him and his friends by providing a home-away-from-home for them.

In what ways is your life similar to Lydia's? Are you worshiping regularly with other believers? Are you attentive and open to the teachings of God's Word? Have you been baptized according to the Lord's command? Are you sharing Christ with other people?

A Magnificent Team for the Lord

And [Paul] found a certain Jew named Aquila...with his wife Priscilla...and he came to them.

ACTS 18:2

*B*ookends. That image comes to mind when we think of Priscilla and her husband, Aquila. This woman and her husband were a magnificent team as they faithfully served God's kingdom.

- *Servants*—Always mentioned together, Priscilla and Aquila stand as a team in marriage and ministry.

- *Itinerants*—Each time this couple is mentioned, they are in a different location. Each city was a key site for ministry.

- *Industrious*—They were tent makers and leather workers.

- *Hospitable*—They opened their hearts and homes.

They took in Paul, and the church in Ephesus met in their home (1 Corinthians 16:19).

- *Persevering*—Expelled from Rome, they knew persecution, yet they remained faithful to the Lord.

- *Knowledgeable*—Priscilla and Aquila listened attentively to Paul as he taught Jews and Greeks alike, gaining the knowledge they needed to serve Jesus.

- *Willing*—This husband-wife duo would do anything, go anywhere, and do whatever for the cause of Christ.

If you are married, you're to support your husband's dreams, hold up your end of the responsibility for family and home, and shoulder your part of the load of life.

If you are single, the pursuit of these godly qualities is important for your faithful ministry and service to the people of God and His kingdom.

Radiant Servanthood

> *I commend to you Phoebe our sister, who is a servant of the church in Cenchrea.*
>
> ROMANS 16:1

Everyone needs help. There is so much to do and so many responsibilities to juggle, not to mention sorrows to bear and ailments to cope with. And the apostle Paul was no different. Second Corinthians 11 lists the many trials he faced. In the face of those trials Paul had the woman Phoebe to help him. Phoebe, meaning "bright and radiant," definitely stands as a shining example of the faithful servanthood God desires in each of us. Three special titles describe her and her faithful ministry.

- *A sister*—Paul called Phoebe "our sister." A devoted and committed member of the family of God, Phoebe was a Christian sister to Paul and the other saints.

- *A servant*—The apostle commended Phoebe as "a servant of the church." The honored title "servant," from which we derive "deacon" and "deaconess," denotes one who serves any and all in the church.

- *A helper*—Paul praised Phoebe, "She has been a helper of many and of myself also." In Greek, "helper" refers to a trainer in the Olympic games who stood by the athletes to see they were properly trained and girded for competition. "Helper" means "one who stands by in case of need."

God's message to us is clear. As is true of all those who love God, you are to be faithful in attendance at church, ready in case a need arises, and willing to meet any needs. Such dedicated, selfless service shimmers in our dark world.

Like Paul, you too can thank God for Phoebe because she most likely delivered the incredible book of Romans to Rome for Paul. As one scholar aptly wrote, "Phoebe carried under the folds of her robe the whole future of Christian theology."[28]

A Godly Heritage

*…genuine faith that is in you, which
dwelt first in your grandmother Lois and
your mother Eunice.*

2 TIMOTHY 1:5

The Scripture passage above pairs the portraits of two outstanding women who loved God—the mother/ daughter team of Lois and Eunice. Here's what we know about Lois.

- *Her name.* Lois' name most likely means "agreeable," and we know the apostle Paul found that to be true.

- *Her background.* A devout Jewess, Lois apparently instructed her daughter, Eunice, and her grandson, Timothy, in the Old Testament scriptures, which prepared their hearts to hear the words about eternal life through Jesus Christ that Paul preached when he passed through their hometown of Lystra (Acts 16:1).

- *Her faith.* Commendations by others show respect

and honor for Lois. Paul saw Lois' faith as genuine and sincere.

- *Her legacy.* Have you heard of Timothy? He was the young Christian who accompanied Paul as he preached the gospel of Jesus and helped establish churches throughout the Mediterranean region. This young man was Lois' grandson and became Paul's true son in the faith, someone Paul could point to as being "like-minded" with himself (Philippians 2:20).

- *Her title.* Many grandmothers are mentioned in the Bible, but Lois is the only one referred to by the honored and revered label "grandmother."

Mothers and grandmothers, you are on assignment to teach God's Word to your children and to your children's children.

Sowing the Seeds of Faith

The genuine faith that is in you, which dwelt first in your grandmother Lois and your mother Eunice.

2 Timothy 1:5

As we consider the portrait of Eunice, the daughter of Lois and the mother of Timothy, you will be surprised by one of the brushstrokes that make up the details of Eunice's daily life—she had an unbelieving husband (Acts 16:1). Eunice was a believing Jewess who shared her faith with her son Timothy, inspiring him to believe in Jesus Christ.

Are you married to a nonbeliever? Do you know women in that position? Be encouraged! If you worry that your children will not discern the truth about Jesus because another belief system and another set of values are represented by their father daily, be assured through Eunice that truth always shines brighter. Also remember your children are "holy," set apart to the Lord by the presence of Christ in you (1 Corinthians 7:14). And because Christ lives in you, Christ lives in your home! That means your children are exposed to a godly witness, whether they want it or not and regardless if they are aware of it. They have divine blessing and protection because of you, their believing mother.[29]

So take heart! Be faithful to sow the seeds of love and divine truth. Be diligent to share the Bible with your little ones. Take every opportunity to pray with them and for them. Share the wonderful stories about Jesus and the specifics about how He became your Savior and can become theirs. Be steadfast in your faith...and in your faith for your children's spiritual development. Above all, live out God's love in your life. And when you're discouraged and it seems your godly efforts for your children are failing, press on remembering that "He who is in you is greater than he who is in the world" (1 John 4:4).

Joining the Family of God

For God so loved the world that He gave His only begotten Son, that whoever believes in Him should not perish but have everlasting life. For God did not send His Son into the world to condemn the world, but that the world through Him might be saved.

JOHN 3:16-17

*H*ow can you become a Christian and join the family of God? John 1:12 says, "As many as received Him, to them He gave the right to become children of God, to those who believe in His name." You need to do two important things.

Believe—Jesus Christ is the living Word of God, and God calls you to acknowledge Him as God-in-flesh and place your faith in Him as Savior and Lord.

Receive—To become a child of God, you must receive Jesus Christ as your personal Savior, acknowledge His death and resurrection on your behalf for your sins, and receive His gift of eternal life with Him.

Have you yielded your life to Jesus Christ? Have you received God's grace gift of salvation and eternal life through Jesus? Believing in Jesus as God-in-flesh and receiving Him into your heart and life by faith places you in to God's family of believers. If you want to take this step of faith now, pray this simple prayer:

Jesus, I am a sinner. But today I am turning away from my sins and following You. I believe You died for my sins and rose again victorious over sin and death. I accept You right now as my personal Savior. Come into my life and help me follow You from this day forward. Thank You!

As you read daily through the pages of the Bible, you will find God's truth, encouragement, excitement, and comfort.

Notes

1. John Milton, Eve.

2. Neil S. Wilson, ed., *The Handbook of Bible Application* (Wheaton, IL: Tyndale House Publishers, Inc., 1992), p. 485.

3. Elizabeth George, *A Woman After God's Own Heart* (Eugene, OR: Harvest House Publishers, 1997), p. 29.

4. Mrs. Charles E. Cowman, *Streams in the Desert*, vol. 1 (Grand Rapids, MI: Zondervan Publishing House, 1965), p. 331.

5. Ben Patterson, *Waiting* (Downers Grove, IL: InterVarsity Press, 1989), p. i.

6. Anne Ortlund, *Building a Great Marriage* (Old Tappan, NJ: Fleming H. Revell Company, 1984), p. 146.

7. Adapted from 1 Corinthians 13:7-8.

8. Lord Dewar.

9. See Judges 4:4; 2 Kings 22:14; Luke 2:36; Acts 21:9.

10. Adapted from principles found in J. Oswald Sanders, *Spiritual Leadership* (Chicago: Moody Press, 1967).

11. Elizabeth George, *Beautiful in God's Eyes* (Eugene, OR: Harvest House Publishers, 1998), pp. 13-16.

12. Julie Nixon Eisenhower, *Special People* (New York: Ballantine Books, 1977), pp. 3-37.

13. Matthew Henry, *Matthew Henry Commentary*, vol. 2, pp. 204-05.

14. Herbert Lockyer, *The Women of the Bible*, (Grand Rapids, MI: Zondervan Publishing House, 1975), pp. 144-49.

15. Ibid, p. 36.

16. Adapted from Herbert Lockyer, *All the Kings and Queens of the Bible* (Grand Rapids, MI: Zondervan Publishing House, 1971), p. 212.

17. Lockyer, *Women of the Bible*, p. 225.

18. Walter B. Knight, *Knight's Master Book of New Illustrations* (Grand Rapids, MI: Wm. B. Eerdmans Publishing Company, 1979), pp. 204-05.

19. Ibid.

20. Ibid.

21. Ibid.

22. The contents of this devotion drawn from Elizabeth George, *Loving God with All Your Mind* (Eugene, OR: Harvest House Publishers, 1994), p. 183.

23. Gien Karssen, *Her Name Is Woman* (Colorado Springs: NavPress, 1975), p. 131.

24. Charles Caldwell Ryrie, *The Role of Women in the Church*, quoted material by Walter F. Adeney (Chicago: Moody Press, 1970), p. 34.

25. William Barclay, *The Gospel of Luke*, rev. ed. (Philadelphia: The Westminster Press, 1975), p. 97.

26. Judson W. Van Deventer, "I Surrender All," hymn, 1896.

27. Joseph H Gilmore, "He Leadeth Me," hymn, 1862.

28. Marvin R. Vincent, *Word Studies in the New Testament*, vol. III, "The Epistles of Paul," quoting Renan (Grand Rapids, MI: Wm. B. Eerdmans Publishing Co., 1973), p. 177.

29. Elyse Fitzpatrick and Carol Cornish, *Women Helping Women* (Eugene, OR: Harvest House Publishers, 1997), pp. 207-19.

Books by Elizabeth George

- 15 Verses to Pray for Your Husband
- Beautiful in God's Eyes
- Breaking the Worry Habit…Forever
- Finding God's Path Through Your Trials
- Following God with All Your Heart
- The Heart of a Woman Who Prays
- Life Management for Busy Women
- Loving God with All Your Mind
- Loving God with All Your Mind DVD and Workbook
- A Mom After God's Own Heart
- A Mom After God's Own Heart Devotional
- Moments of Grace for a Woman's Heart
- One Minute with the Women of the Bible
- One-Minute Inspirations for Women
- Proverbs for a Woman's Day
- Quiet Confidence for a Woman's Heart
- Raising a Daughter After God's Own Heart
- The Remarkable Women of the Bible
- Small Changes for a Better Life
- Walking with the Women of the Bible
- A Wife After God's Own Heart
- A Woman After God's Own Heart®
- A Woman After God's Own Heart®— Daily Devotional
- A Woman's Daily Walk with God
- A Woman's Guide to Making Right Choices
- A Woman's High Calling
- A Woman's Walk with God
- A Woman Who Reflects the Heart of Jesus

Bible Studies

- Becoming a Woman of Beauty & Strength
- Cultivating a Life of Character
- Discovering the Treasures of a Godly Woman
- Embracing God's Grace
- Experiencing God's Peace
- Growing in Wisdom & Faith
- Living with Passion and Purpose
- Nurturing a Heart of Humility
- Pursuing Godliness
- Putting On a Gentle & Quiet Spirit
- Relying on the Power of the Spirit
- Understanding Your Blessings in Christ
- Walking in God's Promises

Study Guides

- Beautiful in God's Eyes Growth & Study Guide
- Following God with All Your Heart Growth & Study Guide
- Life Management for Busy Women Growth & Study Guide
- Loving God with All Your Mind Growth & Study Guide
- Loving God with All Your Mind Interactive Workbook
- A Mom After God's Own Heart Growth & Study Guide
- The Remarkable Women of the Bible Growth & Study Guide
- Small Changes for a Better Life Growth & Study Guide
- A Wife After God's Own Heart Growth & Study Guide
- A Woman After God's Own Heart® Growth & Study Guide
- A Woman Who Reflects the Heart of Jesus Growth & Study Guide
- A Woman's High Calling Growth and Study Guide

Books for Young Women

- Beautiful in God's Eyes for Young Women
- A Young Woman After God's Own Heart
- A Young Woman After God's Own Heart— A Devotional
- A Young Woman's Guide to Discovering Her Bible
- A Young Woman's Guide to Making Right Choices
- A Young Woman's Guide to Prayer
- A Young Woman Who Reflects the Heart of Jesus
- A Young Woman's Walk with God

Books for Tweens

- A Girl After God's Own Heart
- A Girl After God's Own Heart Devotional
- A Girl's Guide to Discovering Her Bible
- A Girl's Guide to Making Really Good Choices
- You Always Have a Friend in Jesus for Girls

Children's Books

- God's Wisdom for Little Boys
- God's Wisdom for Little Girls
- A Little Boy After God's Own Heart
- A Little Girl After God's Own Heart

Books by Jim George

- 10 Minutes to Knowing the Men and Women of the Bible
- 50 Most Important Teachings of the Bible
- The Bare Bones Bible® Handbook
- The Bare Bones Bible® Handbook for Teens
- Basic Bible Pocket Guide, The
- A Boy After God's Own Heart Action Devotional
- A Boy After God's Own Heart
- A Boy's Guide to Discovering His Bible
- A Boy's Guide to Making Really Good Choices
- A Dad After God's Own Heart
- A Husband After God's Own Heart
- Know Your Bible from A to Z
- A Leader After God's Own Heart
- A Man After God's Own Heart
- A Man After God's Own Heart Devotional
- The Man Who Makes a Difference
- One-Minute Insights for Men
- The Remarkable Prayers of the Bible
- You Always Have a Friend in Jesus for Boys
- A Young Man After God's Own Heart
- A Young Man's Guide to Discovering His Bible
- A Young Man's Guide to Making Right Choices

Books by Jim & Elizabeth George

- A Couple After God's Own Heart
- A Couple After God's Own Heart Interactive Workbook
- God's Wisdom for Little Boys
- A Little Boy After God's Own Heart

BIBLE STUDIES *for* BUSY WOMEN

Character Studies

Old Testament Studies

New Testament Studies

About the Author

Elizabeth George is a CBA and ECPA bestselling author of more than 100 books and Bible studies (more than 10 million sold). As a writer and speaker, her passion is to teach the Bible in a way that changes women's lives. For information about Elizabeth's books and to sign up for her newsletter and blogs, please contact Elizabeth at:

www.ElizabethGeorge.com

 goodreads

To learn more about Harvest House books and
to read sample chapters, visit our website:

www.harvesthousepublishers.com

HARVEST HOUSE PUBLISHERS
EUGENE, OREGON